MORE MASSES WITH YOUNG PEOPLE

MORE MASSES

WITH

YOUNG PEOPLE

DONAL NEARY, S.J.

TWENTY-THIRD PUBLICATIONS

Mystic, Connecticut

The publisher acknowledges the permission of the following to quote from copyright material: Jerusalem Bible is copyright © 1966, 1968, Darton, Longman & Todd Ltd and Doubleday & Co Inc.; The Grail Psalms are copyright © 1963, The Grail (England);John Harriot and The Tablet for the reflection on page 28; Conference Book Service and Sylvester O'Flynn OFM Cap. for the reflection on page 32; Wm Collins & Son and William Johnston SJ for the reflection on page 61; Darton, Longman and Todd and Sheila Cassidy for the reflection on page 90.

Twenty-Third Publications
P.O. Box 180
185 Willow Street
Mystic, CT 06355
(203) 536-2611

ISBN 0-89622-419-8

Contents

Introduction

More Masses with Young People presents twenty Masses suitable for young people 16 years of age and older. Mass formulae for the liturgical year are included, along with Masses on themes which are of immediate interest and concern to the young people. This second collection concentrates on those themes, and types of themes, which proved most popular in the first collection, *Masses with Young People,* published in 1985.

These Masses take into account the spiritual development and interests of this age group, and are composed for use in schools, youth groups, and any time a priest or teacher wants to give a group some help in preparing a liturgy. Like most youth resources, they may be used also with older age groups.

An Integral Spirituality
The readings and prayers in these Masses attempt to present an integral approach to liturgical themes. Relationship with God, the Christian way of life, a concern with justice and with relationships with others, are all presented for prayer and reflection. In this way a presentation of liturgical themes is faithful both to the whole gospel and to the needs of young people today.

Using This Book
This book is best used by priests, teachers, and young people together. They may select a theme themselves, or may even pick and choose between readings from different themes. Like any liturgical book, it may be adapted to the age and the level of understanding of the group. The book is for the people, not the people for the book!

The Introduction should be read by a young person, not by the priest if possible. Preparation, as in all liturgical reading, is necessary, as the text is written to be spoken. It is best to work from the principle that everything read at a liturgy should be prepared beforehand. A link is made in the Introduction between the theme of the day and the life and message of Jesus.

Readings are chosen with reference to the theme or the feast. A priest or other leader of the group using these readings needs to reflect on them beforehand, so that the homily or any other presentation after the gospel (e.g. meditation or drama) makes the link between the readings and the theme.

Personal and prayerful reflection from a priest or teacher is particularly relevant for young people. A Communion Reflection is offered; this needs careful preparation and might be read with music in the background. Communion reflections are enhanced by this careful preparation, and by slow and practised reading. Where not otherwise indicated, the Communion Reflections are the composition of the author.

The Alleluia verse has been omitted, following the recommendation of *The Roman Missal* that it is better to omit it when it is not being sung.

I wish to thank staff and students of Mater Dei Institute of Education, Dublin, for their contribution to this book, which has been born largely out of the college's vibrant liturgical life.

Donal Neary SJ

1. BEGINNING THE SCHOOL YEAR

Introduction
This is the Mass to begin our school year. In it we pray for each other, and for the whole school. We'll be asking God's help with our study, our friendships, our sport, our hobbies, and with everything that is part of our school.

We might feel a bit afraid of the coming year, especially if it's an exam year, or if we feel we don't get on too well in the class. Or we can feel very confident and glad to start again. No matter what, we put ourselves before God and ask his help in the coming year.

And we start by being grateful. There are many things to be grateful for in this group. Pause for a moment now and think of something you are thankful for just now. And then think of what else in your life you say thanks for. Be thankful for your interest in and enjoyment of sport, or art, or writing, or dancing, or whatever. Be thankful for your faith, your health, your intelligence, your body, your mind. Be grateful for your friends, for your teachers, for being part of this school. Even though there are always things we don't like about school, there's a lot we'd miss if we weren't here.

Penitential Rite
As we begin our Mass, we ask God's forgiveness for our faults and failings, for our sinfulness and particularly for ways in which we needlessly hurt each other:
You have come to bring us the life of love;
Lord, have mercy.
You have come to bring us the light of truth;
Christ, have mercy.
You plead for us at the right hand of God our Father;
Lord, have mercy.
May almighty God have mercy on us, forgive us our sins, and bring us to life everlasting.

Opening Prayer
Help us, Lord, at the beginning of our school year.
Help us in our work and in our friendships.
We ask this through Christ our Lord.

First Reading   Ephesians 3:14-21

We look ahead to another year. Our first reading is a prayer of St Paul for people he taught. He prays that we grow strong in different areas of our lives. We make this prayer our own for today.

A reading from the letter of St Paul to the Ephesians.

This then is what I pray, kneeling before the Father: In the abundance of his glory may he, through his Spirit, enable your inner selves to grow strong, so that Christ may live in your hearts through faith, and then, planted in love and built on love, with all God's holy people you will have the strength to grasp the breadth and the length, the height and the depth; so that, knowing the love of Christ which is beyond all knowledge, you may be filled with the utter fulness of God. Glory be to him whose power, working in us, can do infinitely more than we can ask or imagine; glory be to him in the Church and in Christ Jesus for ever and ever. Amen.

This is the word of the Lord.

Responsorial Psalm   Psalm 36

A prayer of trust for the coming year

RESPONSE: Be our help, Lord God, in the days to come.

1. If you trust in the Lord and do good,
   then you will live in the land and be secure.
   If you find your delight in the Lord,
   he will grant your heart's desire. R.

2. Commit your life to the Lord,
   trust in him and he will act,
   so that your justice breaks forth like the light,
   and your cause like the noon day sun. R.

Gospel   Mark 4:35–41

When we look to another year, we don't know what's in store; will it be a happy year, a difficult one? The gospel is a story of trusting in the presence of Jesus; as he was present in the apostles' rough times, so he is present always with us.

A reading from the holy Gospel according to Mark.

With the coming of evening that same day, he said to them, 'Let us cross over to the other side.' And leaving the crowd behind they took him, just as he was, in the boat; and there were other boats with him. Then it began to blow a great gale and the waves were breaking into the boat so that it was almost swamped. But he was in the stern, his head on the cushion, asleep. They woke him, and said to him, 'Master, do you not care? We are lost!' And he woke up, and rebuked the wind and said to the sea, 'Quiet now! Be calm!' And the wind dropped, and there followed a great calm. Then he said to them, 'Why are you so frightened? Have you still no faith?' They were overcome with awe and said to one another, 'Who can this be? Even the wind and the sea obey him.'

This is the Gospel of the Lord.

Prayer of the Faithful

Let us make our prayers to God, as we pray at the beginning of our school year:

1. Look after us, Lord, during this coming year; help us live in this school as a Christian community;
R. Lord, hear us.
2. We pray for all who work in our school, for teachers and all its staff; bless them and their families.
R. Lord, hear us.
3. We pray for all past pupils, for those who left last year; we remember especially those who are sick, unemployed, or in any sort of trouble.
R. Lord, hear us.
4. For any of our school who have died: Lord have mercy on them and welcome them home to heaven.
R. Lord, hear us.
5. We pray for people who are new in our school, pupils and teachers; may they be happy here and find friends.
R. Lord, hear us.

Let us pray:
Help us, Lord, to use well the talents you have given each of us.
Help us bring them to our studies
so that we work to the best of our ability.
May we all feel valued, in this school,
for who we are in your sight.
May all we do and learn be in your service,
and in the service of love,

both now and in the future.
We ask this in the name of Jesus our Lord.

Prayer over the Gifts

Lord God, accept our gifts
and see the goodness of your people who offer them to you.
Free us from the influence of evil in our lives
by the power of Jesus who is Lord for ever and ever.

Communion Reflection

What will this year bring?
You do not know; I do not know.
It will bring its usual quota of work and play,
of success and failure, all the things that are part of school life.
It is a new beginning;
the planting of a seed that will grow for a year,
the seed of fruit that will blossom in times to come.

It is a new hope;
hope for good work, for successful results,
for friendship, for fun, for learning.
In this coming year, may there be learning, prayer, and fun.
May there be hard work, faith, and friendship.

May no one in this school be lonely;
may no one be left out in class;
may no one suffer through the others here.

As we begin this year in hope, in prayer and in friendship,
may the Lord begin it with us, be with us during it,
and successfully bring it to its conclusion.

May we, this year, together act justly,
together love tenderly,
and together walk humbly with our God.

Concluding Prayer

May we, who have received the love of God at this Mass,
spread this love wherever we are;
we ask that in this coming year
we spread the love, kindness, and compassion of God in our school.
We make this prayer through Christ our Lord.

2. ASH WEDNESDAY

Introduction

Today we bless ashes and put them on our foreheads. They are reminders of our sinfulness and of our littleness before God.

These ashes were the palms of last Palm Sunday. So they are also ashes of hope. We take them to remind us that we are part of the creation of God. We are made by him, as is the earth and its dust, for life. In taking the ashes we are all equal: men and women, young and old, teacher and pupil; all who work and study in this school are equal in the sight of God. We all take the same ashes.

These ashes have no value except in the sight of God. They are nothing but dust. We are nothing without God: in him we live and move and have our being.

Opening Prayer

Father in Heaven,
the light of your truth gives sight to the darkness of sin.
May this season of Lent bring us the blessing
of your forgiveness and the gift of your light.
Grant this through Christ Our Lord.

First Reading   Joel 2: 13-14

On Ash Wednesday time may be short, as the distribution of ashes will take time. Consider omitting the first reading. If you include it:

A reading from the prophet Joel.

Let your hearts be broken, not your garments torn.
Turn to the Lord your God again,
for he is all tenderness and compassion,
slow to anger, rich in graciousness, and ready to relent.

This is the word of the Lord.

Responsorial Psalm   Psalm 51

A poem of sorrow for sin

RESPONSE: Have mercy on me, God, in your kindness.

1. Have mercy on me, God, in your kindness,
   in your compassion blot out my offence.

O wash me more and more from my guilt,
and cleanse me from my sin. R.

2. My offences truly I know them,
   my sin is always before me.
   Against you, you alone, have I sinned
   what is evil in your sight I have done. R.

Gospel   Mark 1: 14–15

The message of Lent is to change our lives: to be more Christian, more unselfish, more compassionate and kind. This is the beginning of the message of Jesus.

A reading from the holy Gospel according to Mark.

After John had been arrested, Jesus went into Galilee. There he proclaimed the Good News from God. 'The time has come,' he said 'and the kingdom of God is close at hand. Repent, and believe the Good News.'

This is the Gospel of the Lord.

Blessing of Ashes
We ask God to bless these ashes,
which we will use as the mark of our redemption.

Reader 1:
> Dust to dust and ashes to ashes;
> may we remember this day
> that we come from God
> and will go to God.

Reader 2:
> Dust to dust and ashes to ashes;
> may we remember this day
> that we need the Lord's forgiveness.

Reader 3:
> Dust to flowers and ashes to glory:
> may we remember this day
> that Jesus died and rose from death.

Reflection:
> What does it mean that we believe
> that we came from the dust of the earth?
> Not that we were once clay, mud, or dust.

That was a way of saying that we came from God.
It is a way of admitting that we, men and women,
are not masters of ourselves.
We did not call ourselves into being.
We came from the breath and life of God.

Warmth breathing life into nothing,
life growing in the safety of the womb,
life bursting forth as flowers from the earth.

What does it mean that we believe
that we came from the dust of the earth?

What does it mean to be alive?

The same answers:
gift of God,
joy of God,
promise of God.

I am dust;
and flowers grow in dust moistened by the warmth of God.

Prayer over the Gifts
Lord help us to resist the attraction of evil
in the world and in our hearts.
May we give time this Lent to prayer and to good works.
We ask this in the name of Jesus the Lord.

Communion Reflection
Lives in Ashes

Who would say that their lives are in ashes?
People who, through no fault of their own,
have bit the dust of the earth:

who live on the dust of the earth and not in a house,
who squat on the bare earth from whose dust
they have eked out
barely enough food on which to live,
who cry to the dust of the earth for water,
who cry from the ashes of a broken marriage for help,
or children
who look from the dust of abuse, of neglect, of poverty.

Lord, bless them as you have blessed these ashes;
Lord, may we receive them into our lives

as our foreheads received these ashes.

We pray Lord that your living water
may refresh the ashes of our love;
help us to see in each person we meet,
your face, your glory, your delight;
help us to know your cry, your pain, your sorrow
in the faces of all we meet.

Stretch the vision of our eyes
to see in everyone a reflection of God,
of Love, of Joy, of Hope.

Stretch our hearts to love as you do.

Concluding Prayer
Lord, we have shared the sadness of life
by remembering sin and suffering;
we have shared the joy of life in receiving the Eucharist.
Make us always truly thankful,
through Christ Our Lord.

3. LENT 1

Introduction
In this Mass we think of Jesus being led into the wilderness. He was tempted there to go away from the work God wanted him to do. He was tempted by the attraction of power, of wealth, and honour. This was time he spent strengthening himself for his future work: for his preaching, healing, concern for people – work which would lead him to death on the cross. He needed this time to deepen the choices he had already made. He was led into the desert by the Spirit; God wanted him there.

We might think, during the Mass, of the times we have felt we were in the wilderness; when we felt that life was very rough, when we were in conflict with our family, when we were lonely, when we feared failure. He says of himself that he comes looking for us when we feel like that. We ask God for the help to keep doing what we know is right, especially at times when our good intentions may waver.

Penitential Rite
We remember in Lent that our faults can lead us away from God; we also remember that God is all forgiving and all loving. So we ask this forgiveness now for everyone here:
You were led by the Spirit to the desert;
Lord, have mercy.
You were tempted to a life of power and honour and wealth;
Christ have mercy.
You plead with God for us, your people for whom you died;
Lord, have mercy.
May almighty God have mercy on us, forgive us our sins,
and bring us to life everlasting.

Opening Prayer
Lord God,
help us to know what we ought to do in our lives,
to do it with courage and generosity
and always to live in your love.
We ask this through Christ our Lord.

First Reading   Ezekiel 34: 11-16
This is a story of God looking for his people who are lost. It is a story about God being near to us when we feel confused, lonely, misunderstood – any experiences which are like being in a wilderness.

A reading from the prophet Ezekiel.

The Lord says this: I am going to look after my flock myself. As a shepherd keeps all his flock in view when he stands up in the middle of his scattered sheep, so shall I keep my sheep in view. I shall rescue them from wherever they have been scattered during the mist and the darkness. I shall feed them in good pasturage; the high mountains will be their grazing ground. They will rest in good grazing ground; they will browse in rich pastures on the mountains. I myself will pasture my sheep, I myself will show them where to rest: it is the Lord who speaks. I shall look for the lost one, bring back the stray, bandage the wounded and make the weak strong. I shall watch over the fat and healthy. I shall be a true shepherd to them.

This is the word of the Lord.

Responsorial Psalm   Psalm 27

A poem of trust in God

RESPONSE: The Lord is my light and my help.

1. The Lord is my light and my help,
   whom shall I fear?
   The Lord is the stronghold of my life;
   before whom shall I shrink?   R.

2. I am sure I shall see the Lord's goodness
   in the land of the living.
   Hope in him, hold firm and take heart,
   Hope in the Lord!   R.

Gospel   Matthew 3: 1-10

In the wilderness Jesus was tempted to depart from what he knew was his life's mission. He knew confusion, questioning, and also knew that God was with him in the tough times of his own life.

A reading from the holy Gospel according to Matthew.

Jesus was led by the Spirit out into the wilderness to be tempted by the devil. He fasted for forty days and forty nights, after which he was very hungry, and the tempter came and said to him, 'If you are the Son of God, tell these stones to turn into loaves.' But he replied, 'Scripture says: Man does not live on bread alone, but on every word that comes from the mouth of God.' The devil then took him to the holy city and made him stand on the parapet of the Temple. 'If you are the Son of God,' he said, 'throw yourself down, for Scripture says: He will put you in his angels' charge, and they will support you on their hands in case you hurt your foot against a stone.' Jesus said to him, 'Scripture also says: You must not put the Lord your God to the test.' Next, taking him to a very high mountain, the devil showed him all the kingdoms of the world and their splendour. 'I will give you all these,' he said, 'if you fall at my feet and worship me.' Then Jesus replied, 'Be off, Satan! For Scripture says: You must worship the Lord your God, and serve him alone.' Then the devil left him, and angels appeared and looked after him.

This is the Gospel of the Lord.

Prayer of the Faithful
We make our intentions and prayers to God:
1. We ask that we ourselves always know the care of God in the hard-times of our lives;
R. Lord, hear us.
2. For people we know who are in any sort of trouble, particularly members of our own families;
R. Lord, hear us.
3. For young people who are lost, lonely, and confused, we pray they find friendship and a sense of direction in their lives;
R. Lord, hear us.
4. We pray that our faith may grow strong, and that our doubts and difficulties may not bring us away from our interest in God;
R. Lord, hear us.
5. For all who have died, people we know and those of our family, and all who die unmourned, unloved, and unremembered;
R. Lord, hear us.

Let us pray:
God our Father,
hear our prayers which we make in faith, in hope and in love,
through Jesus Christ our Lord.

Prayer over the Gifts
Lord God, accept our gifts of bread and wine.
As we receive from this table the Eucharist of your Son,
help us always to look to you for love,
meaning, and hope in our lives.
We ask this through Christ our Lord.

Communion Reflection

The Wilderness
What does it mean to be led into the wilderness?

To find yourself without bearings,
without direction,
without food, drink, company?

For many
the wilderness is to be without direction.

Not knowing how to find love, meaning, joy in life.
Losing faith, hope, friends, commitment.

This seems to be part of life.

In the wilderness Jesus was tempted
to lose direction and to change his plans.

Can you allow yourself to find refreshment,
faith, self-confidence
when you feel in the wilderness of aloneness
or of failure or confusion?

In your desert
you will know God:
he comes looking for you then.
If you trust and hope
you will know that you are not lost,
for he has come to find you.

It's not that he will bring you to his home
but he will make his home in you.

Concluding Prayer

Lord God,
you have given us the food of life at this table.
Help us always know your friendship in our lives.
In times of sorrow, be our strength
and in times of joy, be our companion.
We ask this through Christ our Lord.

4. LENT 2

Introduction

Our Mass today emphasises the theme of water. Jesus says in the gospel that what he wants to give us is the living water, a fountain or wellspring of life inside us, which is his love.

We'll start our Mass by pouring out a bowl of water. We associate water with life and with growth: we are surrounded by the protection of water in the womb and we need it to grow. We associate it with cleansing and with baptism: we are forgiven and called to follow Jesus in the water of baptism.

We begin our Mass with a prayer of blessing on this bowl of water.

Penitential Rite

This water comes from the earth:
a wellspring of God's creation.
It comes from the clouds and the sky,
made by the living word of God:
We ask you, Lord, to bless this water.
May it be for us a sign of our baptism,
and may it open our hearts and minds to the love of God.
May it also be a sign of forgiveness;
we pour our sins into this water,
and know we are putting them into the forgiving love of Christ.
Grant this through Christ our Lord.

After the blessing of the water each person comes and makes the sign of the cross on his or her forehead; or the bowls can be passed around and each person can make the sign of the cross on the next person's forehead. During this, a song should be sung or some music played.

May almighty God have mercy on us, forgive us our sins, and bring us to life everlasting.

Opening Prayer

Lord God, your love for us is new and strong every day of our lives.
Help us to receive this love into our lives, as the earth receives water.
May your love grow within us,
so that our lives mirror the love you have for your people.
We make this prayer through Christ Our Lord.

First Reading   Isaiah 55:1-3

In this reading God invites his people to welcome his love into their lives. This is an invitation to people who are tired and weary to come to the refreshment of water; an invitation to people, looking for meaning and hope in their lives, to receive it from him.

A reading from the prophet Isaiah.

Oh, come to the water, all you who are thirsty;
though you have no money, come!
Buy corn without money, and eat,
and at no cost, wine and milk.
Why spend money on what is not bread,
your wages on what fails to satisfy?
Listen, listen to me,
and you will have good things to eat and rich food to enjoy.
Pay attention, come to me, listen and your soul will live.

This is the word of the Lord.

Responsorial Psalm   Psalm 95

A poem of joy in God

RESPONSE: Let us give thanks to God all the days of our life.

1. Come, ring out your joy to the Lord,
   greet the rock who saves us.
   Let us come before him, giving thanks,
   with songs let us greet the Lord.   R.

2. Come in, let us bow and bend low;
   let us kneel before the God who made us
   for he is our God and we the people who belong to his pasture,
   the flock that is led by his hand.   R.

Gospel   John 4: 7-14

A lady who is weary of an empty life comes to Jesus, and is offered the friendship of Jesus. This is offered also to us. It is something which will never end. It is a hope and a meaning in our lives which is fuller than any other.

A reading from the holy Gospel according to John.

When a Samaritan woman came to the well where Jesus was, Jesus said to her, 'Give me a drink.' His disciples had gone into the town to buy food. The Samaritan woman said, 'What? You are a Jew, and you ask me, a Samaritan, for a drink?' Jews in fact do not associate with Samaritans. Jesus replied, 'If only you knew what God is offering and who it is that is saying to you: Give me a drink, you would have been the one to ask, and he would have given you living water. Whoever drinks this water will get thirsty again; but anyone who drinks the water that I shall give, will never be thirsty again. The water that I shall give will turn into a spring inside him, welling up to eternal life.'

This is the Gospel of the Lord.

Prayer of the Faithful

As we join together for this Mass, let us pray for each other's intentions:

1. For all our families, parents, brothers and sisters, may the Lord bless them, especially any who are in trouble at the moment.

R. Lord, hear us.

2. For those who are sick, friends or family particularly, may God give them strength in their illness and show his care in the care of others.

R Lord, hear us.

3. For those who work for young people, trying to create employment and those who work with young people who are in any sort of trouble; may the Lord help them in their work.

R Lord, hear us.

4. For those who have died, especially people who are close to us, and those who have died young, as well as those who die in accidents and violence.

R. Lord, hear us.

Let us pray:
God our Father,
hear our prayers
which we make to you in faith, in hope and in love,
through Jesus Christ our Lord.

Prayer over the Gifts

We give you bread and wine
that they may become the life of your Son, Jesus Christ.
We give you ourselves
that we may be filled with the life of Jesus,
the life of love, justice and forgiveness.
We ask this in the name of Jesus the Lord.

Communion Reflection

Who is the woman at the well?
She is the confused person, young or old,
looking for meaning in life,
and wondering where to find it.

Who is the woman at the well?

She is the lonely person,
young, middle aged, old,
who is looking for love,
who has looked for it in the wrong place
or tasted only its pleasures but not its joys.

Who is the woman at the well?

You and me when we fail,
when we hate ourselves,
when we want freedom from our guilt,
when we want light not darkness in our lives,
when we want to know that love can last,
that compassion can heal,
that life is forever.

The truth that Jesus is God and he is a friend,
the truth that love is a mystery and is around us,
the truth that God's love reaches deeply into us
and is a wellspring for ever.

This is the promise of Jesus,
'I will give you living water.'

Concluding Prayer
Lord our God,
in baptism you promised you would always be with us.
We ask you now to help us in everything in our lives,
particularly in study, work, friendship and family.
We make this prayer through Christ our Lord.

5. HOLY WEEK

Introduction
At this time of the year we think of the death of Jesus. His death was the result of the courage of his convictions. He had lived his life with a message of compassion, of equality, of love for the poor, at times criticising the powerful for lording it over the weak. He died at the hands of injustice; everyone connected with his death was in some way covering his own skin. Jesus is an example, like many after him, of the battle of good and evil. And of the battle of love and of selfishness. This battle is fought inside ourselves too, as we live our lives between the attraction of the good and the pull of evil. At the beginning of our Mass we light our candles around the cross and pray that good may overcome evil in our world, that justice may overcome injustice in our land, and that love may overcome selfishness in our own lives.

Penitential Rite
As we prepare to celebrate the Mass, we recall the forgiveness of God in Jesus on the Cross and ask for that forgiveness in our lives:
You forgave everyone from the Cross of your pain and death;
Lord, have mercy.
You promised eternal life to all your people from the Cross;
Christ, have mercy.
You are the One who has overcome the evil of death and of sin;
Lord, have mercy.
May almighty God have mercy on us, forgive us our sins, and bring us to life everlasting.

Opening Prayer
Lord God,
in the death of Jesus your Son,
you have given a sure sign of your love in the world.
Through his death and resurrection,
good has overcome evil.
May we, in our lives, be signs of the victory of good over evil,
peace over war, love over selfishness.
Grant this through Christ our Lord.

First Reading   Phil 2:6-11

This is a hymn of praise to the Lord who suffered at the hands of his people, and who is now at the right hand of God.

A reading from the letter of St Paul to the Philippians.

Jesus' state was divine, yet he did not cling to his equality with God; but emptied himself to assume the condition of a slave, and became as all people are; and being as we all are, he was humbler yet, even to accepting death, death on a cross. But God raised him high and gave him the name which is above all other names, so that all beings in heaven, on earth or in the underworld, should bend the knee at the name of Jesus, and that every tongue should acclaim Jesus Christ as Lord, to the glory of God the Father.

This is the word of the Lord.

Responsorial Psalm   Psalm 22

RESPONSE: My God, why have you deserted me?

1. My God, my God why have you deserted me?
   How far from saving me, the words I groan!
   I call all day, my God, but you never answer,
   all night long I call and cannot rest. R.

2. Here am I, now more worm than man,
   the scorn of mankind, jest of the people,
   all who see me jeer at me,
   they toss their heads and sneer. R.

3. 'If God is his friend, let him rescue him!'
   But God has not despised or disdained the poor man in his poverty,
   has not hidden his face from him,
   but has answered when he called him. R.

Gospel   Luke 23: 44-46

This is the account of the death of Jesus; of the sadness of those who watched it, even of his friends who watched from a distance. The death of Jesus was a lonely death.

A reading from the holy Gospel according to Luke.

It was now about the sixth hour and, with the sun eclipsed, a darkness came over the whole land until the ninth hour. The veil of the Temple was torn right down the middle; and when Jesus had cried out in a loud voice, he said, 'Father, into your hands I commit my spirit.' With these words he breathed his last. When the centurion saw what had taken place, he gave praise to God and said, 'This was a great and good man.' And when all the people who had gathered for the spectacle saw what had happened, they went home beating their breasts. All his friends stood at a distance; so also did the women who had accompanied him from Galilee, and they saw all this happen.

This is the Gospel of the Lord.

Prayer of the Faithful
In our prayers at this Mass we remember people who suffer in the cause of goodness and of right, and who live lives of love and selflessness:
1. We pray for our families, that we may be grateful for the love and the thoughtfulness we show to each other; in this way love is stronger than selfishness;
R. Lord, hear us.
2. We pray for men and women who suffer in the cause of what is right and in obedience to their convictions; in this way truth overcomes a false way of life;
R. Lord, hear us.
3. We pray for people in all parts of the world who are suffering in the cause of equality and of human rights; in this way justice overcomes injustice and good is stronger than evil;
R. Lord, hear us.
4. We pray for people working for peace based on justice, in our own country and in all parts of the world; in this way love overcomes violence and good is stronger than evil;
R Lord, hear us.

Prayer over the Gifts
Lord,
as we offer these gifts of bread and wine,
help us to serve you in prayer and good works.
By our sharing in the Mass during these weeks
may we prepare well to celebrate
the death and resurrection of Jesus Christ our Saviour.
We ask this through Christ our Lord.

Communion Reflection
Pilate

There is too much of Pilate in everyman to be hard on him.
A man of the world might even say
he did not do too badly to hold out so long.
Yet the very familiarity of his behaviour,
the sneaking sympathy it engages
together with its appalling consequences,
is precisely what makes his story so disturbing.
In private, at work, in public office,
the conflict between conviction
and wanting to save one's own skin
runs through life like a dark thread.
The pressures may not be so dramatic,
perhaps only the desire not to seem troublesome,
or too noticeable, or eccentric.
In the everyday world it is easier to be Pilate
than the honest juror.
But for the Christian believer
the figure of Pilate is a perpetually haunting presence,
an uncomfortable reminder
that as well as a clear head and a warm heart,
the Christian needs a strong backbone. *(John Harriot)*

Concluding Prayer
Lord God,
help us in any suffering or sorrow we have.
Help us to know that you care
and feed us with the bread of life.
Give us also a willingness to help others in need.
We ask this through Christ our Lord.

6. EASTER 1

Introduction

We've put flowers around the room for this Mass because it's a Mass about Easter. A key word for Easter is joy. Jesus has said that he came so that we would have joy to the full.

It's worth just asking what sort of joy this is. The joy of succeeding in an exam? The joy of being in love? Or of a good game of football? There are many sorts of joy in our lives: the joy of Jesus at Easter is the lasting joy. After pain, violence, and death he knows now he has overcome it all.

There is no darkness in life that his joy cannot touch. He gives hope in every situation of life: in rejection, in bereavement, in sickness, failure. And in death itself.

Our Mass is a prayer to have some of this joy and to know that it lasts forever, in this life and in the next.

Penitential Rite

Let us ask God's forgiveness for times when we have shown the selfish, un-happy side of ourselves to others, when it could have been otherwise:
Lord Jesus, you said, 'I have come that you may have joy and have it to the full.'
Lord, have mercy.
Lord Jesus, you said to your apostles, 'I leave you peace, my peace I give you.'
Christ, have mercy.
Lord Jesus, you are our risen brother, pleading for us at the right hand of the Father.
Lord, have mercy.
May almighty God have mercy on us, forgive us our sins, and bring us to life everlasting.

Opening Prayer

Almighty God,
may the risen power and love of Jesus Christ
be felt in our lives,
our families, (our school) and our parishes.
May we know it in our country and in our world.
We ask this through Christ our Lord.

First Reading   Acts 2: 22-28

This is a sermon from Peter after the resurrection: he quotes a poem from the bible which expresses the joy of the heart, mind, and body at the sight of God. This was the apostles' joy after the first Easter.

A reading from the Acts of the Apostles.

Then Peter stood up with the Eleven and addressed the crowd in a loud voice: 'Men of Israel, listen to what I am going to say: Jesus the Nazarene was a man commended to you by God, by the miracles and portents and signs that God worked through him when he was among you, as you all know. You killed him, but God raised him to life, for it was impossible for him to be held in the power of death, as David says of him:

I saw the Lord before me always,
for with him at my right hand nothing can shake me.
So my heart was glad, and my tongue cried out with joy;
my body too will rest in the hope
that you will not abandon my soul to Hades,
nor allow your Holy One to know corruption.
You have made known the way of life to me,
you will fill me with joy through your presence.

This is the word of the Lord.

Responsorial Psalm   Psalm 46

A poem of triumph of God over evil

RESPONSE: Lord, you are our victory over evil.

1. God is our shelter, our strength,
   ever ready to help in time of trouble,
   so we shall not be afraid when the earth gives way,
   when mountains tumble into the depths of the sea,
   and its waters roar and seethe. R.

2. Come, think of the marvels of the Lord,
   the astounding things he has done in the world;
   all over the world he puts an end to wars,
   he breaks the bow, he snaps the spear.
   Pause a while and know that I am God,
   exalted among the nations, exalted over the earth. R.

Gospel Luke 24:36-43

The apostles are frightened first at the appearances of Jesus, but eventually they 'are filled with joy.'

A reading from the holy Gospel according to Luke.

They were still talking about all this when he himself stood among them and said to them, 'Peace be with you!' In a state of alarm and fright, they thought they were seeing a ghost. But he said, 'Why are you so agitated, and why are these doubts rising in your hearts? Look at my hands and feet; yes, it is I indeed. Touch me and see for yourselves; a ghost has no flesh and bones as you can see I have.' And as he said this he showed them his hands and his feet. Their joy was so great that they still could not believe it, and they stood there dumbfounded; so he said to them, 'Have you anything here to eat?' And they offered him a piece of grilled fish, which he ate before their eyes.

This is the Gospel of the Lord.

Prayer of the Faithful

Jesus prayed for peace after his resurrection, and that his followers would be people of unity and of forgiveness. Let's make our intentions now in his name:

1. Give us joy, Lord, in knowing that you are always with us, a companion in good times and bad, comfort in our losses;
R. Lord, hear us.
2. Give peace to troubled parts of the world, especially our own country;
R. Lord, hear us.
3. Give hope to people who are down and troubled, especially young people who fear failure and rejection in their lives;
R. Lord, hear us.
4. Give eternal joy to all who have died, especially people in our families and others we know;
R. Lord, hear us.
5. We pray for the sick, the forgotten, the handicapped, the lonely: give them the consolation of your risen power;
R. Lord, hear us.

Let us pray:
God, Creator of everything we love,
hear our prayer which we make in trust in you.
Give us joy and freedom in your risen Son,
Jesus Christ our Lord.

Prayer over the Gifts

May these gifts we offer
be signs of our love for you, Lord God, and for each other.
As you change them into the body and blood of Jesus,
change us too that we become people of joy and hope.
Grant this through Christ our Lord.

Communion Reflection

No End to Hope
We ran then, John and I, uphill,
and I couldn't keep up with his young lungs.
Sure enough, the stone was rolled back.
John peered in but was staying outside. I went right in.
No body! I saw the cloths.
And the cloth for the face was over on its own.
My mind was all confused.
Now, who would take the body
and go to the trouble of taking off the winding cloths?
It was very valuable linen.
John had come in. He was very quiet.
He whispered something. I did not quite catch it at first.
'He is risen! Resurrection, remember!'
I nearly passed out with shock.
'Remember Lazarus ... the day in Naim, remember that girl of Jairus.'
I remembered alright.
Remembered that morning on the lake with the fish.
Remembered waking up that day on the mountain.
Remembered a hundred stunning moments.
How could we have forgotten?
It was we who were in the tomb. We who were in darkness.
And it wasn't a stone in front of the tomb,
but a deep, dark cloud of self pity.
There is no such thing as a tomb unless it is in yourself.
There is never an end to hope.
And in Jesus there is no such thing as death as we used to know it.
(Silvester O'Flynn OFM Cap.)

Concluding Prayer

Bless us, Lord, as we leave the table and the Eucharist of your risen Son.
May we bring with us the hope, peace, and joy
which we find in the resurrection of Jesus
who is Lord, today and forever.

7. EASTER 2

Introduction
In the life of Jesus, after his resurrection, you see him bringing peace, joy, consolation to many different people. When people meet him they know once again that he is alive, and they seem to want to share this good news.

In the Mass today, we try to hear this good news about Jesus: that death and violence and injustice didn't kill him, but that he does his work now in a different way. We are part of his risen life, and the way he works in the world today is through us. Whenever we look after the lonely or the down and out, try to make life's conditions better for people who are in any way deprived, then we are sharing in the work of the resurrection.

The call of the resurrection is to spread faith and justice in our world: faith in Jesus as the word and love of God, and the justice of God, seen in the words and life of Jesus, the risen Lord.

Penitential Rite
Jesus sends his apostles as the Father sent him: to bring reconciliation and justice into the world. Let us ask God's forgiveness for times when we have failed to be people of reconciliation and of justice when it could have been otherwise:
Lord Jesus, you said, 'I have come that you may have joy and have it to the full.'
Lord, have mercy.
Lord Jesus, you said to your apostles, 'I leave you peace, my peace I give you.'
Christ, have mercy.
Lord Jesus, you are our risen brother, pleading for us at the right hand of the Father.
Lord, have mercy.
May almighty God have mercy on us, forgive us our sins, and bring us to life everlasting.

Opening Prayer
Almighty God, may the risen power and love of Jesus Christ
be felt in our lives, our families, (our school) and our parishes.
May we know it in our country and in our world.
We ask this through Christ our Lord.

First Reading   Ephesians 2:17-22

Because of the victory of Jesus over death, we are all united into one community in him. God lives in each of us: that is why we feel the call to share a life of justice and of reconciliation.

A reading from the letter of St Paul to the Ephesians.

Jesus came to bring the good news of peace, peace to you who were far away and peace to those who were near at hand. Through him, both of us have, in the one Spirit, our way to come to the Father. So you are no longer aliens or foreign visitors: you are citizens like all the saints and part of God's household. You are part of a building that has the apostles and the prophets for its foundations, and Christ Jesus himself for its main cornerstone. As every structure is aligned on him, all grow into one holy temple in the Lord; and you, too, in him, are being built into a house where God lives, in the Spirit.

This is the word of the Lord.

Responsorial Psalm   Psalm 119

A poem about Jesus being the foundation of our lives

RESPONSE: Lord, we are glad because of your resurrection from the dead.

1. Give thanks to the Lord, for he is good,
   his love is everlasting.
   Let all God's people say it,
   His love is everlasting. R.

2. The stone which the builders rejected
   has become the corner stone.
   This is the Lord's own work,
   a marvel in our eyes. R.

Gospel   Mark 16: 14-20

The resurrection of Jesus is accompanied by signs of healing and of new life and faith. The risen power of the Lord today brings healing to our society.

A reading from the holy Gospel according to Mark.

Lastly he showed himself to the Eleven themselves while they were at table....He said to them, 'Go out into the whole world; proclaim the good News to all creation....These are the signs which will be associated with believers: in my name they will cast out devils; they will have the gift of tongues; they will pick up snakes in their hands and be unharmed should they drink deadly poison; they will lay their hands upon the sick who will recover.' And so the Lord Jesus, after he had spoken to them, was taken up into heaven: there at the right hand of God he took his place, while they, going out, preached everywhere, the Lord working with them and confirming the word by the signs that accompanied it.

This is the Gospel of the Lord.

Prayer of the Faithful

Jesus prayed for peace after his resurrection, and that his followers would be people of unity and of forgiveness. Let's make our intentions now in his name:

1. Give us joy, Lord, in knowing that you are always with us, a companion in good times and bad, comfort in our losses;
R. Lord, hear us.
2. Give peace to troubled parts of the world, especially in our own country;
R. Lord, hear us.
3. Give hope to people who are down and troubled, especially young people who fear failure and rejection in their lives;
R. Lord, hear us.
4. Give eternal joy to all who have died, especially people in our families and others we know;
R. Lord, hear us.
5. We pray for the sick, the forgotten, the handicapped, the lonely: give them the consolation of your risen power.
R. Lord, hear us.

Let us pray:
God, Creator of everything we love,
hear our prayer which we make in trust in you.
Give us joy and freedom in your risen Son,
Jesus Christ our Lord.

Prayer over the Gifts

May these gifts we offer
be signs of our love for you, Lord God, and for each other.
As you change them into the body and blood of Jesus,
change us too that we become people of joy and hope.
Grant this through Christ our Lord.

Communion Reflection

Raise Your People

Where is the Lord?
Gone away?
His work finished?

How are his followers?
Separating?
Their hopes finished?
He is with God.
He is raised to God,
not just raised by God or in God,
but brought on high to God.

He lives now in the place where he was before time began:
with the Father.

He lives with God
and he is found in his people;
to be found among people is to be found with God.

Where do we find the One who is with God?
In Galilee, on the road to Emmaus, at the seaside.
Among people.

Lord, help me to notice you,
follow you, enjoy you, embrace you, in your people.
Risen Lord, raise your people!

Concluding Prayer

Bless us, Lord,
as we leave the table and the Eucharist of your risen Son.
May we bring with us the hope, peace and joy
which we find in the resurrection of Jesus who is Lord,
today and forever.

8. ON BEING A CHRISTIAN

Introduction

Our Mass today is on the theme of being a Christian. We want to pray and think over the essentials of following Christ.

One main aspect of our Christianity is that we try to look on the world as Jesus did. A word that sums up Christianity is love. This is how Jesus would distinguish his disciples. Many people look on Christianity in different ways: stressing prayer, social action, sacraments, devotions and morality. All are important, but none more important than love. Jesus showed this in his life.

Michel Quoist, a French writer, puts it well: 'What distinguishes the Christian from the non-Christian? Nothing. The Christian is no better or no worse; he is no more virtuous than the others; in fact he might even be less so. No more loving or giving than anyone else; there are people who love more. There's only one difference: as a Christian you believe that God loves you and that if you welcome this love, it will be transmitted to the world through you, and on this love the world will be built.'

Penitential Rite

Jesus asks us to confess that we are people who fail to love, and asks us to allow God's forgiveness into our lives:
Lord Jesus, you are the Truth of God our Father;
Lord, have mercy.
Lord Jesus, you are the Life of forgiveness and reconciliation;
Christ, have mercy.
Lord Jesus, you are the Way to love and joy;
Lord, have mercy.
May almighty God have mercy on us, forgive us our sins, and bring us to life everlasting.

Opening Prayer

Lord God,
make us truly grateful for the gift of our faith in you.
It gives hope and meaning to our lives.
Deepen our Christianity, and help us to share it.
We ask this through Christ Our Lord.

First Reading   Hebrews 10:19-25

This reading stresses different aspects of being a Christian.

A reading from the letter of St Paul to the Hebrews.

Through the blood of Jesus we have a right to enter the sanctuary, by a new way which he has opened for us. And we have the supreme high priest over all the house of God. So as we go in, let us be sincere in heart and filled with faith, our minds sprinkled and free from any trace of bad conscience and our bodies washed with pure water. Let us keep firm in the hope we profess, because the one who made the promise is faithful. Let us be concerned for each other, to stir a response in love and good works. Do not stay away from the meetings of the community, as some do, but encourage each other to go.

This is the word of the Lord.

Responsorial Psalm   Psalm 111

A poem of trusting in God and giving to the poor

RESPONSE: We thank you Lord for the gift of our faith.

1. Happy the man who fears the Lord,
   who takes delight in his commands;
   his children will be blessed on earth;
   the children of the upright will be blessed. R.

2. Open handed he gives to the poor;
   his justice stands firm for ever.
   His head will be raised in glory. R.

Gospel   John 15: 12-17

In this gospel Jesus sums up the Christian message in three aspects: love of each other, bearing fruit in our lives, and knowing God.

A reading from the holy Gospel according to John.

This is my commandment: love one another as I have loved you. A man can have no greater love than to lay down his life for his friends. You are my friends if you do what I command you. I shall not call you servants any more, because a servant does not know his master's business. I call you friends, because I have made known to you everything I have learned from my Father. You did not choose me, no, I chose you; and I commissioned you to go out and to bear fruit, fruit that will last.

This is the Gospel of the Lord.

Prayer of the Faithful

With thanks to God, let us pray and make our intentions to him:

1. As we thank the Lord for the gift of faith, we pray for an increase of faith and love in our own lives;
R. Lord, hear us.
2. We ask God's help and care for people, especially young people, who find it difficult to believe. Help them in their doubts;
R. Lord, hear us.
3. We pray for people who are in prison or suffering any oppression because of their efforts to spread the gospel of Jesus;
R. Lord, hear us.
4. We pray for anyone who has helped in giving us the gift of faith and of Christianity: our parents, teachers, friends;
R. Lord, hear us,
5. We pray for priests, sisters, brothers and all who are ministers of religion. May the Lord bless them in their work;
R. Lord, hear us.

Let us pray:
Lord God, deepen within us our faith in you.
Give us joy in the efforts of Christians,
all over the world, to spread your gospel.
We ask this through Christ our Lord.

Prayer over the Gifts

May our small gifts of bread and wine, Lord God,
be the gifts of our hearts.
Make us joyful in your love of us,
and intent on giving the world your gospel of love
and of reconciliation.
We ask this in the name of Jesus the Lord.

Communion Reflection

Real Christianity

In the different churches throughout the world,
there are many people trying to spread the gospel;
in different ways:

teaching people to pray and to make sense of their lives,
beginning projects which help the developing countries,

collecting money at home for the poor and the needy.
This is the work of the Church:
to help people find God in prayer, and so bring God's light to them,
to be concerned with building a just society,
and so bring God's love in places of need,
to pass on to the young the faith and gospel of Jesus
and so bring hope and meaning to life.

The desire to do the work of Jesus in the world
is born in joy and in thanks:
joy that God has become one of us,
thanks that God has asked us to work with him.

Help us, Lord, to be real Christians,
truly people of your love in the world.

Help us to act justly,
love tenderly,
and walk humbly with you,
for that is what the Lord God asks us to do.

Concluding Prayer
We go from this place, Lord God,
strengthened by the body and blood of Jesus.
In the Eucharist,
may we always know your love and your call in our lives.
Thank you for being so close to us.
We make this prayer through Christ our Lord.

9. THE THIRD WORLD 1

Introduction

In this Mass we're going to pray for people in the third world, and for people who are working there to better conditions. We've all seen pictures on TV and in the papers of hunger, starvation, homelessness, and the utter misery millions of people live in.

These are children of God, brothers and sisters of Jesus Christ; they are also our brothers and sisters because of him.

Our prayer is insincere unless we try to do something. So we'll also do something during the week to raise some money for a third world group and send it to them.

But can we also feel some of the pain felt by people who are hungry, without homes, without water, without access to education? We ask God that we may also have some of the sense of urgency of Jesus Christ in face of the huge inequalities in our world.

We'll begin the Mass by listening to what a few people, who have lived in poorer countries, have said:

Gandhi said:

'The earth has enough for everyone's need, but not enough for everyone's greed.'

Niall O'Brien, an Irish priest in the Philippines, writes:

'The joint arms budget for 1987/88 has touched on 900 billion dollars. Enough to put food on the table daily of every hungry person in the world. Yet that money is set aside for death, to kill, to maim, to destroy, to create more hunger and destruction and frequently precisely to put down the revolutions caused by hunger, to silence the cry of the poor.'

Penitential Rite

With hope, we ask God's forgiveness for the inequality in the world:
You came to your own people and they did not receive you;
Lord, have mercy.
You died on the Cross for the sins of the world;
Christ, have mercy.
You plead for us at God's right hand;
Lord, have mercy.
May almighty God have mercy on us, forgive us our sins, and bring us to life everlasting.

Opening Prayer

Lord God, deepen our conviction
that each man and woman in the world
is created in your image and likeness.
Help us all to work for the dignity of each person.
We make this prayer through Christ our Lord.

First Reading   Galatians 3: 26-29

*In these lines Paul the apostle states that there are no distinctions of na-
tionality or religion in the eyes of God. The same is true of wealth and
poverty: all are children of God.*

A reading from the letter of St Paul to the Galatians.

You are all of you, children of God through faith in Jesus Christ. All
baptised in Christ, you have all clothed yourselves in Christ, and there
are no more distinctions between Jew and Greek, slave and free, male
and female, but all of you are one in Christ Jesus.

This is the word of the Lord.

Responsorial Psalm   Psalm 22

Prayer of people in great need

RESPONSE: The Lord hears the cry of the poor; blessed be the Lord.

1. My God, my God why have you forsaken me?
   You are far from my prayer and the cry of my plea.
   I call to you all the day long,
   from my terrors set me free. R

2. Do not stand aside, O Lord.
   My strength, come quickly to my help;
   rescue my soul from the sword,
   save me from the lion's mouth;
   then I will proclaim your name to my people,
   praise you in the assembly of your people. R

Gospel   Luke 2: 6-8, 15-17

*We remember that Jesus on his birth was poor and homeless; in the lives of
many millions of people he is still poor and homeless.*

A reading from the holy Gospel according to Luke.

While they were at Bethlehem, the time came for her to have her child, and she gave birth to a son, her first born. She wrapped him in swaddling clothes and laid him in a manger, because there was no room for them in the inn.... Now when the angels had gone from them into heaven, the shepherds said to one another, 'Let us go into Bethlehem and see this thing that has happened which the Lord has made known to us.' So they hurried away and found Mary and Joseph, and the baby lying in the manger.

This is the Gospel of the Lord.

Prayer of the Faithful

1. We pray for those who suffer from starvation; may those of us who have plenty be generous in our support of them;
R. Lord, hear us.
2. We pray for people all over the world who are homeless, and ask the blessing of the Lord on all efforts to give people a home;
R. Lord, hear us.
3. We pray for people who are in prison;
R. Lord, hear us.
4. We pray for all those who work for the people of the third world, for their efforts to create a better life for others, and ask that we be sensitive to injustice in our own country;
R. Lord, hear us.
5. We ask that we may feel the pain that God feels at the tragedies of injustice, hunger, and want in our world;
R. Lord, hear us.

Let us pray:
God,
give us eyes like yours, which see the want of the world,
a heart like yours, which feels for the cry of innocent people,
and a willingness to do our best
to make things better for people in need.
We ask this through Christ our Lord.

Prayer over the Gifts

As we offer gifts of bread and wine,
may we also offer our own time and interest
in trying to help people in need.
We make this prayer through Christ our Lord.

Communion Reflection

Faces of the World

Think of some faces of the world,
faces you have seen on the street of the city,
on the TV screen or in the newspaper.

The woman nursing the starving child,
an old man evicted from a flat,
a young person imprisoned for protest against injustice;
the factory where kids of ten are working;
men and women walking for miles in the desert for food,
shanty towns as the rain sweeps hundreds of huts away;
refugees pushed from one place to another.

Jesus says:
whatever you do for my people, you do for me.
And whatever you fail to do for my people, you fail to do for me.
This means wherever people are hungry, I am hungry,
wherever people are homeless, I am homeless,
wherever people are exploited, I am exploited.

Lord God, forgive us.
Lord God, make us feel for people as you feel.
Lord God, encourage us to help those in need.

Concluding Prayer

As we have received from this table, Lord God,
the food of life and the bread of our salvation,
we ask that we may become in our world
the compassion, forgiveness and justice of Jesus your Son,
who is Lord forever and ever.

10. THE THIRD WORLD 2

Introduction

The subject of our Mass today is the third world, with the idea that in many situations people are poor, and are kept poor, so that others stay rich and get richer.

For example, much of what we use in the West is kept cheap by child labour in the factories of the third world.

In cities, different social classes are kept apart by town planners.

The laws of apartheid are a systematic way of keeping down a certain group of the population.

Emigration, with its ensuing problems, may, in fact, be part of an economic plan.

The cost of education is a way of keeping education within the access of the wealthy only, and so the spiral goes on and on.

Our Mass today is a Mass for forgiveness: asking God's forgiveness for the ways in which we live which keep many nations and peoples poor and deprived. The oppressed and those who are poor, through no fault of their own, are the special friends of God.

We need to become aware of systems of greed and how we take part in them. We ask at this Mass that we become sensitive to the ways in which people are suffering through no fault of their own, and to ways in which economic and political systems keep them down. And we pray that we may become increasingly aware that in the cry of every oppressed person—man, woman, or innocent child—is heard the cry of Jesus in his people today.

Penitential Rite

We ask God's forgiveness and love, as we join in this Mass:
Lord Jesus, you say that whatever we do to any of your people, we do to you;
Lord, have mercy.
Lord Jesus, you have come to call the nations to repentance;
Christ, have mercy.
Lord Jesus, you call us to generosity in your service from the throne of heaven;
Lord, have mercy.
May almighty God have mercy on us, forgive us our sins, and bring us to life everlasting.

Opening Prayer
Lord God, give us and all your church
a real desire for better conditions
for the millions of starving and poor people in the world.
We ask that we may be aware of their needs,
in our own country and in the whole world.
Grant this through Christ our Lord.

First Reading   Isaiah 1: 10-17

This is a hard reading about God's reaction to sacrifices and prayers that don't also involve care for the needy.

A reading from the prophet Isaiah.

'What are your endless sacrifices to me?' says the Lord. 'I am sick of holocausts of rams and the fat of calves. Bring me your worthless offerings no more, the smoke of them fills me with disgust. New Moons, sabbaths, assemblies, I cannot endure festival and solemnity. Your New Moons and your pilgrimages I hate with all my soul. You may multiply your prayers, I shall not listen. Your hands are covered with blood, wash, make yourselves clean. Take your wrongdoing out of my sight. Cease to do evil, learn to do good, search for justice, help the oppressed, be just to the orphan, plead for the widow. 'Come now, let us talk this over,' says the Lord. 'Though your sins are like scarlet, they shall be white as snow; though they are red as crimson, they shall be like wool.'

This is the word of the Lord.

Responsorial Psalm   Psalm 94

A poem about the love of God for justice

RESPONSE: The Lord is close to the brokenhearted.

1. You never consent to that corrupt tribunal
   that imposes disorder as law,
   and takes the life of the virtuous
   and condemns the innocent to death. R.

2. No, the Lord is still my citadel,
   my God is a rock where I take shelter;
   he will pay them back for all their sins,
   he will silence their wickedness. R.

Gospel

This story of Jesus is a serious reflection on the differences in our world. Lazarus is a symbol of the poor, Dives of the unsympathetic rich person. There is no doubt where Jesus' sympathies lie.

A reading from the holy Gospel according to Luke.

Jesus said to his disciples, 'There was a rich man who used to dress in purple and fine linen, and feasted magnificently every day. And at his gate there lay a poor man called Lazarus, covered with sores, who longed to fill himself with the scraps which fell from the rich man's table. Dogs even came and licked his sores. Now the poor man died and was carried away by the angels to the bosom of Abraham. The rich man also died and was buried.

'In his torment in Hades he looked up and saw Abraham a long way off with Lazarus in his bosom. So he cried out, "Father Abraham, pity me and send Lazarus to dip the tip of his finger in water and cool my tongue, for I am in agony in these flames." "My son," Abraham replied, "remember that during your life good things came your way, just as bad things came the way of Lazarus. Now he is being comforted here while you are in great agony. But that is not all: between us and you a great gulf has been fixed to stop anyone crossing from your side to ours." The rich man replied, "Father, I beg you then to send Lazarus to my father's house, since I have five brothers, to give them warning so that they do not come to this place of torment too." "They have Moses and the prophets," said Abraham, "let them listen to them." "Ah no, Father Abraham," said the rich man, "but if someone comes to them from the dead they will repent." Then Abraham said to him, "If they will not listen either to Moses or the prophets, they will not be convinced even if someone should rise from the dead."'

This is the Gospel of the Lord.

Prayer of the Faithful

As a prayer of the faithful, prepare bowls of rice and pass them around to each person: this is the total food for a day for many millions of people in our world. Each person prays silently over the bowl of rice. Spontaneous intentions might be made at the end of the rice prayer.

Prayer over the Gifts

Put some symbols of the suffering world on the altar: a cross of nails, a rice bowl, a crucifix, a symbol of medical needs, and any other such symbols, saying the following prayer:

Lord God,
we offer these to you as gifts of our love for your people.
We offer them in sadness, in anger,
but in compassion and love.
As you come to us in bread and wine,
may you come to us also in justice for your people.
We ask this through Christ our Lord.

Communion Reflection

Lord, forgive!
Forests, needed for the native economy in a debt-ridden third world nation, have been cut down to give the raw material for food cartons to be cheaply made for the first world. Lord, forgive us.

Children of five and six are working ten hours or more a day in a hot factory of an Indian city to make bangles for the wealthy and profit for someone who never knows their conditions. Lord, forgive us.

A young man in South Africa cannot go where he wants, work where he is qualified, all because he is black. Lord, forgive us.

A Dublin girl of sixteen is refused a job because she has the 'wrong address.' Lord, forgive us.

A priest is in a labour camp because he wants to profess his faith; a woman is in prison for getting involved in the struggle for justice. Lord, forgive us.

This now might lead into some spontaneous reflections for forgiveness.

Concluding Prayer

May we know ever more clearly, Lord God,
that you are especially close to us
when we suffer and when we work for those who suffer.
Give us hearts like yours,
that we may act justly,
love tenderly,
and walk humbly with you in our lives.
We ask this through Christ our Lord.

11. VOCATION 1

Introduction
Vocation could be called 'partnership with Christ'; it is a partnership in his work in the world. Working for peace and for justice is the work of Jesus in the world; so is trying to improve the quality of family life, to achieve human rights for people, to start employment schemes, to collect money for poorer countries and for groups of people who are poor. The work of Jesus is seen in our friendships and ways we try to help different people.

The risen Jesus is still present and at work in the world; our hands, our service, our hearts, are the ways in which he works.

Vocation is a calling from God to partnership. We'll pray over that now; we'll ask for a deep sense within ourselves of being called by God into this partnership. Often we don't believe that we can do something good for God; we suffer from a lack of confidence, but God can use each of us, as God used each of the apostles in his service.

Penitential Rite
Lord, have mercy.
Christ, have mercy.
Lord, have mercy.
May almighty God have mercy on us,
forgive us our sins,
and bring us to life everlasting.

Opening Prayer
Lord God,
each of us has gifts and talents.
We thank you for these.
We ask you that we may use them in your service.
We ask this in the name of Jesus the Lord.

First Reading
Jeremiah 1: 4-10

This is an account of a call in the bible: Jeremiah is called by God, he knows his own weakness and resists the call, but God promises him his help. Working with God is always like that: it seems too much for a person, but we can only do our best little by little.

49

A reading from the prophet Jeremiah.

The word of the Lord was addressed to me, saying:
'Before I formed you in the womb I knew you;
Before you came to birth I consecrated you;
I have appointed you as a prophet to the nations.'
I said, 'Ah, Lord; look, I do not know how to speak: I am a child!'
But God replied,
'Do not say, "I am a child."
Go now to those to whom I send you
and say whatever I command you.
Do not be afraid of them,
for I am with you to protect you –
it is the Lord who speaks.'
Then the Lord put out his hand and touched my mouth and said to me:
'There! I am putting my words into your mouth.
Look, today I am setting you
over nations and over kingdoms,
to tear up and to knock down,
to destroy and to overthrow,
to build and to plant.'
This is the word of the Lord.

Responsorial Psalm   Psalm 117

RESPONSE: Go out to the whole world and proclaim the gospel of the Lord.

1. Praise the Lord, all you nations,
   praise him, all you peoples. R.

2. Strong is his love for us,
   He is faithful for ever. R.

Gospel   John 20: 19-21

We hear the words of the risen Lord about being sent. That is what vocation entails: God sends us into partnership with Jesus to spread his gospel in whatever way we can.

A reading from the holy Gospel according to John.

In the evening of that same day, the first day of the week, the doors were closed in the room where the disciples were, for fear of the Jews. Jesus came and stood among them. He said to them, 'Peace be with you,' and showed them his hands and his side. The disciples were filled with joy when they saw the Lord, and he said to them again, 'Peace be with you.

As the Father sent me,
so I am sending you.'

This is the Gospel of the Lord.

Prayer of the Faithful

In our prayers at this Mass we will pray for people in the different vocations within the church:

1. For fathers and mothers, who are called by the Lord to share his love in families; for our own parents, that the Lord God bless them and help them;
R. Lord, hear us.
2. For priests and religious, for those we know in our parishes and our schools, may God give them all the help they need in their work of helping others;
R. Lord, hear us.
3. For men and women working away from home for the gospel of the Lord, especially young people on voluntary work. Be with them, Lord, when they are lonely and finding times hard;
R. Lord, hear us.
4. For young people everywhere, for everyone in this group, we pray that we live our lives in partnership with Christ and be an influence for good on each other;
R. Lord, hear us.
5. Give each person here a desire to do good in their lives, and to try as best they can to bring Jesus Christ to others;
R. Lord, hear us.

Let us pray:
God, you call us into your service.
Give us happiness in doing what is right,
and in trying to help others.
Help us to know that true happiness is in giving what we can
to you and to your people.
We ask this in the name of Jesus the Lord.

Prayer over the Gifts

Lord God,
receive the good desires we have to serve you,

as you receive our bread and wine.
May the compassion and the love of Jesus shine in our lives.
We ask this in his name, Jesus the Lord.

Communion Reflection
'What can I do?'
Respect that question.
Trust that you,
one man, one woman,
can do for God what otherwise would not be done.

Trust that some people will hear the gospel of Jesus,
that some who are in need
will find the touch of human love,
that others will find a listening ear
or a voice in their poverty,
only because you have chosen
to give God a central place in your life ...

It is not just your work,
your choice,
your decision.
You choose because you are chosen,
you choose because
in the heart of your desire to love,
you have found the heart of God searching for you.
(Come, Follow Me. Pastoral of the Irish Bishops, 1989)

Concluding Prayer
Lord God,
we receive the friendship of Jesus
when we receive his Body and Blood.
We also hear his call to be his partners in bringing love,
peace and justice to the people he loves.
Help us to give ourselves to what you want,
and to help you fulfil your plans for the world.
Grant this through Christ our Lord.

12. VOCATION 2

This Mass is particularly suitable for use at a Vocations Workshop.
It can, of course, be adapted for use on other occasions.

Introduction

Our prayer at Mass today is for light and clarity, now or in the future,
about our vocation. Each of us has a question at some depth about the
possibility of priesthood or religious life for us. We want, each of us, to
do the best thing in our lives for God and for his people. We trust that
whatever way God calls us is what will be best for each of us; God looks
into our hearts, knows us and invites us on a way of discipleship which will
bring out the best in each person, and in which each person can give of
his or her best for God.

We are here these days to think, to pray, and to talk together about
our questions; we are here to ask to know God's will in our lives. In our
Mass we hear the word of God and pray for each other: for light to
know what God is asking of each of us, courage to follow it, and trust to
believe that this way will bring joy in our own lives and to people we
meet and work for in the future.

Penitential Rite

As we prepare to celebrate the mystery of God's love in our lives, we ask
his forgiveness for sinfulness and selfishness:
You have called us from death into life;
Lord, have mercy.
You have called us from darkness into your own light;
Christ, have mercy.
You are pleading for us at the right hand of the Father;
Lord, have mercy.
May almighty God have mercy on us,
forgive us our sins,
and bring us to life everlasting.

Opening Prayer

God our Father,
you have been with us
on our way to this point of decision in our lives.
Give us light to know what your call in our lives is
and courage to do what you ask.
We make this prayer through Christ our Lord.

First Reading   Philippians 3:7-14

Paul writes here of his one desire in life: to know Jesus Christ in his death and resurrection, and to spend his life in companionship with him. This is the true meaning of priesthood and religious life.

A reading from the letter of St Paul to the Philippians.

Because of Christ I have come to consider all advantages that I had as disadvantages. Not only that, but I believe nothing can happen that will outweigh the supreme advantage of knowing Christ Jesus, my Lord. For him I have accepted the loss of everything, and I look on everything as so much rubbish if only I can have Christ, and be given a place in him. I am no longer trying for perfection by my own efforts, the perfection that comes from the Law, but I want only the perfection which comes through faith in Christ, and is from God and based on faith. All I want is to know Christ and the power of his resurrection and to share his sufferings by reproducing the pattern of his death. That is the way I can hope to take my place in the resurrection of the dead. Not that I have become perfect yet: I have not yet won, but I am still running, trying to capture the prize for which Christ Jesus captured me. I can assure you I am far from thinking I have already won. All I can say is that I forget the past and I strain ahead for what is still to come. I am racing for the finish, the prize to which God calls us upwards to receive in Christ Jesus.

This is the word of the Lord.

Responsorial Psalm   Psalm 27

A poem of trust in the Lord and a request to know his way

RESPONSE: Show us your pathway, Lord God, for our lives.

1. The Lord is my light and my help;
   whom shall I fear?
   The Lord is the stronghold of my life;
   before whom shall I shrink? R.

2. Do not abandon or forsake me,
   O God my help!
   Instruct me, Lord, in your way,
   on an even path lead me. R.

Gospel

The call of Jesus is a call to service. This comes out in the story from Mark's gospel where Jesus compares his work in the world with the work of the 'famous': his is the way of service.

A reading from the holy Gospel according to Mark.

When the other ten heard this they began to feel indignant with James and John, so Jesus called them to him and said to them, 'You know that among the pagans their so-called rulers lord it over them, and their great men make their authority felt. This is not to happen among you. No, anyone who wants to become great among you must be your servant, and anyone who wants to be first among you must be slave to all. For the Son of Man himself did not come to be served but to serve, and to give his life as a ransom for many.'

This is the Gospel of the Lord.

Prayer of the Faithful

Let us pray to God for our intentions as we gather together in the name of Jesus the Lord:

1. Give us clarity, Lord, to know your will, courage to do what we know is your will, and always a deep love of you and of your people;
R. Lord, hear us.
2. Give us joy always, Lord, in doing what is right in our lives; help us to know you as the God of life and of joy;
R. Lord, hear us.
3. We pray for priests and religious everywhere: especially for those working in situations in which their religious commitment puts them in danger;
R. Lord, hear us.
4. For all who have helped us in our life of faith, for our parents, family, and friends, may the Lord bless them;
R. Lord, hear us.

Let us pray:
Lord God, you have called us into your service.
Give us joy and delight in knowing you and loving you;
give us courage to do what is best for each of us.
We ask this through Christ our Lord.

Prayer over the Gifts
Lord God,
your Son offered himself on the Cross for love of your people.
May we share in his risen work
of inviting others into the love you have for your people.
Make us men and women of strong faith in your service.
We ask this through Christ our Lord.

Communion Reflection
The call of the Lord brings out the best in each person.
A young man or woman
who follows the call of the Lord
in priesthood or religious life
will grow in openness and humanity
in this way of life.

The call of Jesus
is for life and life more abundant.
Do you find a leap of joy in thinking of priesthood,
an excitement in giving your life as a religious?

Like the sunrise after the darkness,
or the sunshine after rain,
or reconciliation after bitterness.
This is real joy, change, newness.

The call of the Lord is felt in the joy of the heart,
and in the desire to be like him in the world.
It's felt also in deep trust:
his faithfulness is like the lighthouse in the fog,
the smile of companionship in times that are tough,
the touch of a hand in the dark.

Lord, give me trust to believe in your faithfulness,
courage to follow what is best and right in my life,
and joy in knowing that real life is life in your company.

Concluding Prayer
Lord God,
as we go from this table strengthened
and nourished by the bread of life,
we ask that we can be this bread of life among your people.
We make this prayer through Christ our Lord.

13. CARE FOR THE EARTH 1

Introduction
You can look on creation in different ways. Some people use the earth's resources for good, others for selfish purposes. We can be horrified at the way forests have been cleared to make huge profits for industry, thus resulting in floods and starvation. Or how water and air have been polluted.

The earth has been given to us by God to be cared for, treasured, enjoyed, used for the benefit of all his people. Jesus was a lover of the earth, and saw the finger of God his Father in all of creation.

At Mass today, we give thanks for the earth. We pray for God's forgiveness for the way we misuse the earth, and we pray that we may be truly grateful for it and treat it well.

Penitential Rite
We ask God's mercy and pardon, particularly for ways in which we, his people, misuse the earth:

God of the earth,
God of the fire,
God of the fresh waters,
God of the shining stars,
Heavenly Father, have mercy on us.

God who made the world,
God of the many tongues,
God of the nations,
God of golden goodness,
Heavenly Father, have mercy on us.   *(from the Irish)*

May Almighty God have mercy on us,
forgive us our sins,
and bring us to life everlasting.

Opening Prayer
Lord God, you created everything and you saw that it is good.
Help us to care for what you have made,
for the earth, for our rivers, for our beaches,
for all the resources of the earth,
and to use them that people may live in dignity and in safety.
We ask this through Christ our Lord.

First Reading   Colossians 1:15-18

Everything created is created in Jesus Christ; all of our world can remind us of him. This song of praise is about that: and if we sing in joy for all creation, then how could we not but treat it well?

A reading from the letter of St Paul to the Colossians.

He is the image of the unseen God,
the first born of all creation,
for in him were created all things
in heaven and on earth:
everything visible and everything invisible,
all things were created through him and for him.
He exists before all things
and in him all things hold together,
and he is the Head of the Body,
that is, the Church.

This is the word of the Lord.

Responsorial Psalm   Psalm 8

A poem of praise and joy for all God's creation

RESPONSE: How great is your name, O Lord, our God, through all the earth.

1. When I see the heavens, the work of your hands,
   the moon and the stars which you arranged,
   what are we that you should keep us in mind,
   or your children that you care for us? R.

2. Yet you have made us little less than gods,
   with glory and honour you crown us,
   give us power over the work of your hands,
   put all things under our feet. R.

3. All of the sheep and cattle,
   yes, even the savage beasts,
   birds of the air and fish
   that make their way through the waters. R.

Gospel   Matthew 6: 25-34

Jesus looks at God's creation and is full of thanks. He asks his disciples to look at all God has made, how he cares for it, and see that he cares even more for his people.

A reading from the holy Gospel according to Matthew.
I am telling you not to worry about your life and what you are to eat, nor about your body and what you are to wear. Surely life is more than food and the body more than clothing! Look at the birds in the sky. They do not sow or reap or gather into barns, yet your heavenly Father feeds them. Are you not worth much more than they are.... Do not worry; do not say, 'What are we to eat? What are we to drink? What are we to wear?' ... Set your hearts on God's kingdom first, and on God's saving justice, and all these other things will be given you as well.
This is the Gospel of the Lord.

Prayer of the Faithful
Let us pray to the Lord who loves all he makes.
We ask him for our intentions at this Mass:
1. Be with all those who care for your creation: people who work for the preservation of the environment, people who give time to keeping the world beautiful to live in;
R. Lord, hear us.
2. Give us the sensitivity to work so that everyone has an equal share of the world's resources, especially space for a home and food for the table;
R. Lord, hear us.
3. Help us to see the beauty of God in the beauty of the world;
R. Lord, hear us.
4. Help us to be angry at the damage done to creation, at pollution of our seas and forests, and at all other sorts of damage to the environment;
R. Lord, hear us.

Let us pray:
Lord, you are the creator of all in the world,
and you hate nothing of what you create.
Give us a love for your world,
give us a sense that we are to care for this world.
We ask this through Christ our Lord.

Presentation of the Gifts
Symbols of creation could be brought to the altar, and, in silence, placed with the bread and wine.

Or, alternatively, put a small mound of earth in the sanctuary with plants, fruit, water, and other symbols of creation in it. Put there also the bread and wine and let them be taken from there to the altar while saying the Prayer over the Gifts.

Prayer over the Gifts
Lord God, from the many gifts you give us,
we place this bread and wine on your altar.
We know that many people badly need ordinary food and drink,
as all of us need the food and drink
which you give us in this sacrament.
Make us caring people like your Son, Jesus Christ our Lord.

Communion Reflection
God's Creation
Be open to this mysterious and obscure sense of presence.
God is there: in the mountains and the ocean,
in the flowers and the birds,
in the trees and the fields.
Walk through green fields or the brown bog,
walk beside the ocean, listening to every sound,
aware of the beauty
and, above all,
conscious of the enveloping presence
that hovers over everything.
This can be exhilarating prayer.
For God is wonderfully present in all things,
working in all things, giving himself to us in all things.
We cannot see him or touch him;
but we can sometimes sense his presence:
his healing presence.
When your mind and heart are troubled,
walk and look at nature.
Feel the air and the rain washing your body
and cleansing your spirit.
Eat and drink copiously
from the energising, liberating, healing, life-giving table of life.
(William Johnston SJ, Being in Love [Collins 1988])

Concluding Prayer
As we go from this table of your word
and the communion of your love,
may we bring with us, Lord God,
an appreciation of the beauty of all you make,
and especially a strong faith in the unique beauty of each person
who is made in your image and likeness.
We ask this through Christ our Lord.

14. CARE FOR THE EARTH 2

Introduction

You can look on creation in different ways. Some people use the earth's resources for good, others for selfish purposes. We can be horrified at the way forests have been cleared to make huge profits for industry, thus resulting in floods and starvation. Or how water and air have been polluted.

The earth has been given to us by God to be cared for, treasured, enjoyed, used for the benefit of all his people. At Mass today, we give thanks for the earth. We pray for God's forgiveness for the way we misuse the earth, and we pray also that we may be truly grateful for it and treat it well.

Penitential Rite

As we celebrate the love of God in Jesus Christ, let us ask God's forgiveness for our sins and sinfulness:
Lord you have given us the wonders of the world for the enjoyment of your people;
Lord, have mercy.
You have asked us to use well the resources of the earth;
Christ, have mercy.
You are the Son of God who walked and loved our earth, now with God forever.
Lord, have mercy.
May Almighty God have mercy on us,
forgive us our sins,
and bring us to life everlasting.

Opening Prayer

Lord God, we thank you for the earth.
Give us a love for all you have created;
a love for the earth,
a love for the sea,
a love for our cities.
Give us, above all, a love for your people,
created in your own image.
We ask this through Christ our Lord.

First Reading   Psalm 104

This is a song of praise to God for all he has made. When we praise him for the earth and the whole world, we can ask ourselves how we, his people, use the earth.

A reading from the book of Psalms.

Praise the Lord, my soul,
Lord my God, how great you are!
Clothed in majesty and splendour,
wearing the light as a robe.

You fixed the earth on its foundations;
in the ravines you opened up springs,
running down between the mountains;
from your high halls you water the mountains,
satisfying the earth with the fruit of your works:

for cattle you make the grass grow,
and for people the plants they need,
to bring forth food from the earth,
food to make them sturdy of heart.

How countless are your works, O Lord,
all of them made so wisely.

This is the word of the Lord.

Responsorial Psalm   Psalm 8

A poem of praise for God's creation

RESPONSE: How great is your name, O Lord, our God, through all the earth.

1. When I see the heavens, the work of your hands,
   the moon and the stars which you arranged,
   what are we that you should keep us in mind,
   or your children that your care for us? R.

2. Yet you have made us little less than gods,
   with glory and honour you crown us,
   give us power over the work of your hands,
   put all things under our feet. R.

3. All of the sheep and cattle,
   yes, even the savage beasts,
   birds of the air and fish
   that make their way through the waters. R.

Gospel

Jesus uses food, one of God's greatest created gifts, as a way of showing the generosity and love of God. The food he gives here is a way of describing the care of God for his people. All of God's creation is for the use and benefit of all his people. As we hear this gospel we are reminded that the food of the earth is for everyone. And then we wonder why so many are starving.

A reading from the holy Gospel according to Matthew.

When evening came, the disciples went to him and said, 'This is a lonely place, and time has slipped by; so send the people away, and they can go to the villages to buy themselves some food.' Jesus replied, 'There is no need for them to go: give them something to eat yourselves.' But they answered, 'All we have with us is five loaves and two fish.' So he said, 'Bring them to me.' He gave orders that the people were to sit down on the grass; then he took the five loaves and the two fish, raised his eyes to heaven and said the blessing. And breaking the loaves he handed them to his disciples, who gave them to the crowds. They all ate as much as they wanted, and they collected the scraps left over, twelve baskets full.

This is the Gospel of the Lord.

Prayers of the Faithful
As we pray this Mass, let us make our intentions to God:
1. We pray for people all over the world who are hungry; help us to use all the resources of the world to feed them;
R. Lord, hear us.
2. We pray for all who are sick, especially children; help us to use all our medical resources for the benefit of all God's people;
R. Lord, hear us.
3. We pray for people who have no homes; we pray that the space of the world be equally shared so that all have shelter;
R. Lord, hear us.
4. We pray for ourselves: that we get sufficiently enthused about the hunger, homelessness, and poverty of our people to do something about it in our lives;
R. Lord, hear us.
5. We pray for all who work against nuclear disaster; instead of weapons of destruction, may the world come to see the sense of spending resources so that people may live in dignity and peace;
R. Lord, hear us.

Let us pray:
Lord God,
you have come to feed the hungry, give refreshment to the thirsty,
heal the sick, make your home among your people.
Give us the power to work for a world
that shares its resources more justly with all people.
Grant this through Christ our Lord.

Presentation of the Gifts

Symbols of creation could be brought to the altar, and in silence placed with the bread and wine.

Prayer over the Gifts

Lord God, from the many gifts you give us,
we place this bread and wine on your altar.
We know that many people badly need ordinary food and drink
as all of us need the food and drink
which you give us in this sacrament.
Make us like your Son, Jesus Christ our Lord.

Communion Reflection

'There lives the dearest freshness deepdown things.'

What would come to mind?
A daffodil blowing in the wind?
A feather caught in the gate of a sheepfold?
Earth, damp and strong?

And you feel you're part of all God's creation
and all is very good.

A joy to believe in God the Creator,
a joy to partake in creation:
a child's first smile,
an old man's gentle hardworked hand,
the air you breathe,
the water that refreshes:

The peace of God,
the life of Christ,
the joy of the Spirit.

'There lives the dearest freshness deepdown things.'

What else might come to mind?

The smog that darkens a city,
the river polluted and fish killed,
the napalm burns on a child's back,
the young man or girl near the bomb at the wrong time,
the garden vandalised just for the hell of it?

And you dread being part of all that,
part of the destruction of what God has planned,
all that is very good is for our stewarding.

Father, forgive the violence that shatters your peace;
Jesus, forgive our neglect of life,
Spirit, forgive the destruction of beauty that we cause.

Father, thank you for the peace of your creation,
Jesus, thank you for the life you bring,
Spirit, thank you for the beauty of your life.

Concluding Prayer
As we go from this table of your word
and the communion of your love,
may we bring with us, Lord God,
an appreciation of the beauty of all you make,
and especially a strong faith in the unique beauty
of each person who is made in your image and likeness.
We ask this through Christ our Lord.

15. CARE FOR FAITH

Introduction

'Faith is a gift from God, as fragile as a flower in the desert that needs to be watered and cultivated. This cultivation is even more important in a society and culture that tend to speak less and less about faith.'

The way we think about God, and our prayer, changes as we get older. We get new questions, and experiences in life make us ask different things of God. Sometimes people panic that they are losing their faith when in fact their faith is growing. It's something like friendship or any relationship: what we were happy about as children doesn't satisfy us in the teens, and what is a good friendship in the teens won't satisfy us in adult life.

We can sometimes go very negative about faith. Different people can give a bad impression of Christianity. But that shouldn't keep anyone from growing towards God themselves. Our faith is affected by the faith and lives of others, but it is an intensely personal experience. Jesus himself got to know God gradually in his life: through the Jewish religion, through his mother and Joseph. He got to know the God inside himself.

We pray at this Mass that our faith may be honest, sincere, and open to growth. And we pray for the faith of each person here, that it can be a life-giving relationship in their lives.

Penitential Rite

As we prepare to celebrate the mystery of God's love, we ask his forgiveness and love in our lives:
You are the Way to true life and to God in heaven;
Lord, have mercy.
You are the Truth of our questions and the love of God;
Christ, have mercy.
You are the Life of God and the meaning of human life;
Lord, have mercy.
May almighty God have mercy on us,
forgive us our sins,
and bring us to life everlasting.

Opening Prayer

Help our faith to grow, Lord God.
We ask that we may know you
as the Way, the Truth, and the Life.
Grant this through our Lord Jesus Christ.

First Reading

Colossians 3:1-4

The life of faith is a life focused on God, and looking at the world the way God sees the world. It is mysterious; we will only fully know God in the life that is to come.

A reading from the letter of St Paul to the Colossians.

Since you have been brought back to true life with Christ, you must look for the things that are in heaven, where Christ is, sitting at God's right hand. Let your thoughts be on heavenly things, not on things that are on the earth, because you have died, and now the life you have is hidden with Christ in God. But when Christ is revealed, he is your life and you too will be revealed in all your glory with him.

This is the word of the Lord.

Responsorial Psalm

Psalm 86

A prayer for the care of God

RESPONSE: Lord I believe, help my unbelief.

1. Listen to me, Lord my God, and answer me,
   poor and needy as I am; keep me safe,
   I am your devoted one,
   save your servant who relies on you. R.

2. You are my God, take pity on me,
   Lord, I pray to you all day long;
   give me reason to rejoice,
   for to you, Lord, I lift up my soul. R.

Gospel

Luke 2:41-52

In this story Jesus loses his father and mother and finds God himself; but he also returns with them to their home and finds God there also. Faith is a personal search for God and his truth and love within a community of believers.

A reading from the holy Gospel according to Luke.

Every year his parents used to go to Jerusalem for the feast of the passover. When he was twelve years old, they went up for the feast as usual. When they were on their way home after the feast, the boy Jesus stayed behind in Jerusalem without his parents knowing it. They assumed he was with the caravan, and it was only after a day's journey that they went to look for him among their relations and acquaintances. When they failed to find him there they went back to Jerusalem looking for him everywhere.

Three days later, they found him in the Temple, sitting among the doctors, listening to them and asking them questions; and all those who heard him were astounded at his intelligence and his replies. They were overcome when they saw him and his mother said to him, 'My child, why have you done this to us? See how worried your father and I have been, looking for you.' 'Why were you looking for me?' he replied, 'Did you not know that I must be busy with my father's affairs?' But they did not understand what he meant.

He then went down with them and came to Nazareth, and lived under their authority. His mother stored up all these things in her heart. And Jesus increased in wisdom, stature, and in favour with God and people.

This is the Gospel of the Lord.

Prayer of the Faithful
We bring our prayers to God in faith and trust that he hears what we ask:
1. Deepen our faith; help us to be honest in our questions and humbly to accept that we don't have all the answers;
R. Lord, hear us.
2. Give faith and hope to young people who are confused; we pray that we can help our friends in times when they feel lost and abandoned;
R. Lord, hear us.
3. Give courage and strength to people who are imprisoned or oppressed in any way because of their faith in you;
R. Lord, hear us.
4. For people who to help others in their life of faith, particularly our parents and teachers;
R. Lord, hear us.

Let us pray:
Lord God, we pray these intentions of our hearts.
We believe in your care for us.
Help us remember this all the days of our life.
We ask this through Christ our Lord.

Prayer over the Gifts
We bring these gifts of bread and wine in faith to you;
we know that they come from you, source of all life.
May they bring us to a loving faith in your care for us.
We ask this through Christ our Lord.

Communion Reflection
Faith: Dependency on God

If Jesus said, 'Blessed are the poor in spirit,'
it was because of his conviction,
born out of his own life
and learned through the experience of men and women he met,
that the poor in spirit are blessed, content, and happy.

Maybe he listened for hours to a woman
who was humble and open about her lack of success and prestige,
but found her happier than many a society lady of leisure,
because she had found the meaning of her life in God and in love;
or maybe he spent time with a man who grappled with frailty
or struggled with a weakness like alcoholism,
and realised that deep down this man had a contentment
in a humble approach to his own weakness;

and he knew that his own fulfilment and contentment
was in being totally dependent on his Father
for life, love, happiness, perseverance, and a sense of purpose ...

then he could say,
'I live, as I was born, poor in spirit, and I am blessed.'

Concluding Prayer
God our Creator and Father,
may our minds be open to the Truth we hear in Jesus,
may our hearts be open to his Life,
and may our feet be guided always on his Way,
the path of faith on our journey of life.
We ask this through Christ our Lord.

16. CARE FOR FAMILY

Introduction
Our family life is one of the most important and significant areas of our lives. Family life can bring great happiness or unhappiness to us and this Mass is a time to pray for our families.

We're thankful for the care and love we get in our families. At times, we don't always experience that love and care, so we pray for any families which are in difficulties.

We learn a lot about life in our families: the first people we love and quarrel with are in the family. We learn how to get on with others, how to deal with frustrations, how to give and take in day to day life at home.

No family is completely happy; every family has its problems. But it is our beginning, our rock, our security. We move away from family as we get older. But the family is the starting point, and, in the normally content family, the place to which we come back for home, for love, for a place to stay.

Jesus himself grew up in a family with Mary and Joseph and an extended family of cousins, aunts, and uncles, who must have played a large role in his life. In this Mass we pray for our parents, our brothers and sisters, and that each of us can, in his or her own way, help the happiness of our own family life.

Penitential Rite
As we begin our Mass, we ask God's forgiveness for sin; especially selfishness at home, ways in which we have hurt our parents, sisters and brothers.

Lord Jesus, you are Son of God and son of Mary;
Lord, have mercy.
Lord Jesus, you are word made flesh, one of the family of humankind;
Christ, have mercy.
Lord Jesus, you are our brother at the right hand of God our Father;
Lord, have mercy.
May almighty God have mercy on us,
forgive us our sins,
and bring us to life everlasting.

Opening Prayer

Lord God, creator of all who live,
you sent your Son among us
to gather us together as brothers and sisters;
he grew up in the family of Mary and Joseph.
We ask his help in our family life;
may we know contentment, peace, and happiness in our families.
We ask this through Christ our Lord.

First Reading   Colossians 3:12-15,17

This is an ideal of the qualities of family life.

A reading from the letter of St Paul to the Colossians.

As the chosen of God, then, the holy people whom he loves, you are to
be clothed in heartfelt compassion, in generosity and humility, gentle-
ness and patience. Bear with one another; forgive each other if one of
you has a complaint against another. The Lord has forgiven you; now
you must do the same. Over all these clothes, put on love, the perfect
bond. And may the peace of Christ reign in your hearts, because it is for
this that you were called together in one body. Always be thankful.
Whatever you say or do, let it be in the name of the Lord Jesus, in
thanksgiving to God the Father through him.

This is the word of the Lord.

Responsorial Psalm   Psalm 127

RESPONSE: The Lord provides for all his family.

1. If the Lord does not build the house,
   in vain do the builders labour;
   if the Lord does not watch over the city,
   in vain does the watchman keep vigil. R.

2. Truly children are a gift from the Lord,
   a blessing, the fruit of the womb.
   Indeed the children of youth
   are like arrows in the hand of a warrior. R.

Gospel   Luke 1: 39-45

*In the simplicity of a family scene with Mary and Elizabeth, both expect-
ing a child, God visits his people. It is in our families that we first hear of
God and we first experience love and care.*

A reading from the holy Gospel according to Luke.

Mary set out at that time and went as quickly as she could to a town in the hill country of Judaea. She went into Zechariah's house and greeted Elizabeth. Now as soon as Elizabeth heard Mary's greeting, the child leapt in her womb and Elizabeth was filled with the Holy Spirit. She gave a loud cry and said, 'Of all women, you are the most blessed and blessed is the fruit of your womb. Why should I be honoured with a visit from the mother of my Lord? For the moment your greeting reached my ears, the child in my womb leapt for joy. Yes, blessed is she who believed that the promise made her by the Lord would be fulfilled.'

This is the Gospel of the Lord.

Prayer of the Faithful
Let us make our intentions to God now, praying especially for our families and for the good of family life:
1. We pray for our parents, living and dead; may the Lord reward them always for all they do and have done for us;
R. Lord, hear us.
2. We pray for our sisters and brothers; may we grow to love and understand each other in our family life, and try quickly to overcome our differences and quarrels;
R. Lord, hear us.
3. For all our families, we pray; and for any families we know where there is sickness or unemployment;
R. Lord, hear us.
4. For those in families who suffer through bad relationships, through any difficulties parents may have or have had in the past; for those whose families, for any reason, have broken up, we pray for the healing power of the Lord;
R. Lord, hear us.
5. For any of our family who have emigrated; may they find work, happiness, and contentment in their new country;
R. Lord, hear us.

Let us pray:
May love, peace and contentment grow, Lord God, in our families;
may we learn to understand each other's difficulties and strains.
Give us the grace of forgiveness and tolerance for each other.
We ask this through Christ our Lord.

Presentation of the Gifts

Bring up symbols of family life – a photo album, some staple food, a key, a picture of grandparents – anything which would remind the group of family during the Mass.

Prayer over the Gifts

We give to you Lord, these small gifts of bread and wine.
They are our invitation to you to be part of our family life,
for they are signs of your love for us.
May we who offer these gifts offer also our service to you.
Grant this through Christ our Lord.

Communion Reflection

The Family of Jesus

The Lord Jesus has known the joys and sorrows of family life:
living for many years with Mary and Joseph,
he learned the joy of closeness with parents,
the joy of getting to know them and help them,
the joy of their love.

He knew too the sorrow of death when Joseph died;
and that his parents knew hardship because of him,
    forced as they were, out of their homeland when he was born,
    letting him go from them in the temple at Jerusalem,
    and Mary would see him suffering and dying on a Cross.
He left home, knowing his mission in life,
and Mary, the mother who loved him,
had to learn to let him go,
to love others and do the work of God,
being his mother in a new way.

The Word became one of us:
fully one of us, the son of a family:
the Son of God shared our family life.

Concluding Prayer

As we go from this place, Lord God,
where we have celebrated the love of Jesus your Son,
we ask you to bless us and all those we love.
May all we do and say
be words and deeds which Jesus would see as his.
Grant this through Christ our Lord.

17. CARE FOR FRIENDSHIP

Introduction
In this Mass we thank God for the friends we have, and we pray for them. Friendship is something all of us want, and all of us look for. In friendship we share our lives with another, we are there in good times and bad. We can help another in trouble, and share successes and joy.

Life without friends is a lonely life, and many find it like that. We need to care for our friends, to give them time by being together with them, to talk together, have fun. Friendship doesn't grow automatically. It grows with time spent together, with forgiveness after fall outs and misunderstandings. It grows also in the trust that we are accepted by another.

God is the source of friendship, and when we have found a friend, we share in the life of God. Friends come and go; we part when we move locality, school, or we can sometimes drift apart. But we can always be thankful for our friends, and the part they play in our lives.

At this Mass let's pray that all of us can grow in our capacity to be friends, now and in the future.

Penitential Rite
The Mass is the love of God made visible in Jesus Christ, who calls us his friends. Let us ask God's forgiveness for our sins:
You call us friends because you have made yourself known to us;
Lord, have mercy.
You are Son of God and friend of everyone;
Christ, have mercy.
You are with God, our friend, in the kingdom of heaven;
Lord, have mercy.
May almighty God have mercy on us,
forgive us our sins,
and bring us to life everlasting.

Opening Prayer
Lord God, you are the source of all friendship.
Help us be good friends to each other;
help us also to offer friendship, when we can,
to those who are lonely or in need.
We make this prayer through Christ our Lord.

First Reading

I Corinthians 13: 4-8

The qualities of love in this letter of Paul are the qualities of a good friend-ship.

A reading from the first letter of St Paul to the Corinthians.

Love is always patient and kind; it is never jealous;
love is never boastful or conceited; it is never rude or selfish;
it does not take offence, and is not resentful.
Love takes no pleasure in other people's sins,
but delights in the truth;
it is always ready to excuse,
to trust, to hope and to endure whatever comes.

This is the word of the Lord.

Responsorial Psalm

Psalm 139

God is a true friend who knows you through and through.

RESPONSE: We thank you for the wonder of friendship.

1. Lord, you search me and you know me,
   you know my resting and my rising,
   you discern my purpose from afar. R.

2. For it was you who created my being,
   knit me together in my mother's womb,
   I thank you for the wonder of my being,
   for the wonders of all your creation. R.

Gospel

John 15:12-17

Friendship is how Jesus looks on his relationship with his disciples, and this is how he thinks of each of us too.

A reading from the holy Gospel according to John.

A man can have no greater love than to lay down his life for his friends. You are my friends if you do what I command you. I shall not call you servants any more, because a servant does not know his master's business; I call you friends, because I have made known to you everything I have learnt from my Father. What I command you is to love one another.

This is the Gospel of the Lord.

Prayer of the Faithful

Let us now make our intentions to God, who calls us friends:

1. We pray for our friends; may the Lord bless them and give them joy;
R. Lord, hear us.
2. We pray that we can be open to making friends with many kinds of people, and notice in our class that everyone has a need for friends;
R. Lord, hear us.
3. We pray for people who find it difficult to make friends, who find it difficult to trust or to be honest with people;
R. Lord, hear us.
4 For those who are lonely, especially young people who find themselves turning to drink, drugs, or superficial relationships to give themselves a sense of meaning in their lives;
R. Lord, hear us.
5. For everyone who has shown love to us in our lives;
R. Lord, hear us.

Let us pray:
Lord God, from you comes every good gift,
and we thank you for the gift of friendship.
Help us to learn to be people who can trust,
be honest and be faithful in our friendships.
We ask this through Christ our Lord.

Presentation of the Gifts

Symbols of friendship might be placed on the altar at the Preparation of the Gifts: a letter, a ring, a candle, or other symbols that would suggest friendship to the group.

Prayer over the Gifts

Lord God, friend of your people,
friend of the world, friend of the earth:
be with us as we journey together in life to you.
May this bread and wine
always remind us of your friendship
in Jesus Christ our Lord.

Communion Reflection

Thanks for Friendship

I think of people I met in the past.

A friend in primary school: we used to play trains together;
a girl in third year when I first fell in love;
a university friend who shared the same courses.

Many, many people.
Where are they now?
Some are still friends, others just a Christmas card;
others no longer met but never forgotten.
Not every friendship lasts forever;
we move house, school and job,
we drift away from people,
but every memory of friendship shared,
even for a short time,
is a treasure,
like sunshine and warmth in our lives,
like a cool breeze on a humid day,
like a shower of rain refreshing the earth.

Thank you, Lord,
for the gift of friendship
at every time of life.

Concluding Prayer
Lord God, in Jesus you give us your own friendship.
We thank you for this gift.
Help us to cherish it and nourish it,
and never demean it for anyone.
Make us true friends
in the name and the spirit of Jesus our Lord.

18. CARE FOR LIFE

Introduction
Our theme for this Mass is care for life. The best word to describe God's creation is life, and it is the most precious of gifts. People obviously go to great lengths to save, preserve, and cherish life. We would go to great lengths to save our own life; and, when we hear of someone whose burden of life was so great that he or she committed suicide, we feel a great sympathy.

Life can also be treated cheaply: killings in war, violence in many parts of the world, kidnapping, imprisonment, abortion. These are ways in which human life is devalued and is looked on as having less than its real value.

Jesus valued life: He enjoyed the life of the earth, of all creation and, above all, treated each person with the dignity due to everyone. He said he came on earth that 'we might have life and have it to the full.'

So we pray at this Mass that human life be valued everywhere, and that we ourselves may always value human life above all political, financial, and other concerns.

Penitential Rite
As we offer this Mass, we ask God's forgiveness for ways in which we have failed to value life as God himself does:
Lord Jesus, you come among us that we have life and have it to the full;
Lord, have mercy.
Lord Jesus, you give us the life of God in word and sacrament;
Christ, have mercy.
Lord Jesus, you promise us the fulness of life in the presence of God our Father for all eternity;
Lord, have mercy.
May almighty God have mercy on us, forgive us our sins, and bring us to life everlasting.

Opening Prayer
Lord God, all life comes from you.
It is your gift to us.
In gratitude for the gift of life,
we pray that your people everywhere
may value each human life as one precious in your eyes.
We ask this through Christ our Lord.

First Reading
Wisdom 11: 24-12:1

A reading from the Book of Wisdom.

Lord, you love everything that exists, and nothing you have made disgusts you, since, if you hated something, you would not have made it. And how could a thing subsist, had you not willed it? Or how be preserved, if not called forth by you? No, you spare all, since all is yours, Lord, lover of life! For your imperishable spirit is in everything.

This is the word of the Lord.

Responsorial Psalm
Psalm 34

A poem about the care God has for us: He is creating us all the time.

RESPONSE: Lord, we thank you for the gift of life.

1. The eyes of the Lord are on those who revere him,
   on those who rely in his love,
   to rescue their souls from death,
   and keep them alive in famine. R.

2. Our soul waits for the Lord,
   he is our help and our shield;
   our hearts rejoice in him,
   we trust in his holy name.
   Lord, let your love rest on us,
   as our hope has rested in you. R.

Gospel
Luke 7:1-17

Jesus valued the gift of life: He spoke of having life to the full. This story from the gospel is a sign of his wish that we, his people, be fully alive in love, in care, and in hope for ourselves and each other.

A reading from the holy Gospel according to Luke.

It happened soon afterwards he went to a town called Nain, accompanied by his disciples and a great number of people. Now when he was near the gate of the town there was a dead man being carried out, the only son of his mother, and she was a widow. And a considerable number of the townspeople was with her. When the Lord saw her he felt sorry for her and said to her, 'Don't cry.' Then he went up and touched the stretcher, and the bearers stood still, and he said, 'Young man, I tell you, get up.' And the dead man got up and began to talk. And Jesus gave him to his mother.

This is the Gospel of the Lord.

Prayer of the Faithful

As we pray about the gift of life, let us make our intentions to God:

1. Give us always, we pray, a love for life: for the life of the earth, for animal life and above all for human life;
R. Lord, hear us.
2. Forgive the sins against life; sins of violence, murder, abortion, and any ways in which the gift of life is not respected;
R. Lord, hear us.
3. For those who work in the service of life: for doctors, nurses, hospital staffs, especially in parts of the world where a lot of illness occurs through neglect of life and lack of food and water;
R. Lord, hear us.
4. Help your people, Lord, to work for the fulness of life: that people everywhere may have enough to eat, to wear, and a home for themselves and family;
R. Lord, hear us.
5. Give eternal life to all, especially young people, who have died;
R. Lord, hear us.

Let us pray:
Lord, you are the source of life.
We ask that we may be always truly grateful for the gift of life,
and see you as the Lord of life.
We ask this through Christ our Lord.

Presentation of the Gifts
Symbols of life are brought to the altar: e.g. plants, fish in a bowl, some earth with a flower in it, food, pictures of reconciliation, joy, love.

Prayer over the Gifts
Lord our God, from the gifts of life you have given us,
we now give you bread and wine.
We do this in thanks for all you have given us.
May they become the greatest of your gifts,
the body and blood of Jesus our Lord.

Communion Reflection
The Gift of Life
Think of some pictures of life:

a father with a newborn child,
a mother teaching her child,
friends talking together,
a band playing music,
people dancing, playing sport, talking together;
this is a share in the life of God.

The glory of God is man and woman fully alive:
alive to the love among us,
alive to life growing in the earth and under the sea,
alive also in suffering, in pain and sorrow,
knowing that the life of God uplifts us then.

God, thank you for the gift of life;
for the ways we bring each other alive,
for the ways we share physical life,
emotional support, and spiritual hope.

Lord, we pray,
let us be,
like you,
lovers of life.

Concluding Prayer
We have received, Lord God,
the bread of life from this table.
May we always treasure and enjoy the gift of life,
and bring new life to those we meet.
We make this prayer through Christ our Lord.

19. CARE FOR SELF

Introduction

This could seem a selfish title for a Mass! But God has a special sort of care for us that he offers us. He asks us to care for ourselves as he cares for us.

It's like as if every person started off as a canvas to be painted or a photo to be developed – just as God compares himself making us, in Scripture, to a potter making a vase. Each of us is called to make something good of the given self: to care and look after ourselves so that God's life can grow in us.

People care for themselves in different ways: eating the right foods, educating themselves, nurturing the life of friendship, caring for their relationship with God in prayer and the sacraments.

They don't look after themselves when, for example, they drink too much, get into idleness, fail to see themselves as valuable in the sight of God and therefore worth taking care of.

We'll pray in this Mass about taking care of ourselves. And if you take real care of yourself, you'll find yourself wanting to take care of others.

Penitential Rite

My brothers and sisters,
as we prepare to offer the Mass together,
we ask God's forgiveness for our sins,
particularly if we have failed to take right care of ourselves:

Lord Jesus,
you grew in knowledge and wisdom in your own life;
Lord, have mercy.

Lord Jesus,
you call us to be with you all the days of our life;
Christ, have mercy.

Lord Jesus,
you are our brother and friend at the right hand of God our Father;
Lord, have mercy.

May almighty God have mercy on us,
forgive us our sins,
and bring us to life everlasting.

Opening Prayer

Lord God, you have loved each of us and known each of us
from the first moment of our existence.
You have valued us, rejoiced in us, the people whom you love.
As you care for us, help us care for ourselves.
As we care for ourselves, help us care for each other.
We ask this through Jesus Christ, our Lord.

First Reading   Isaiah 62: 2-4

*If you hear these words of God in Isaiah, you'll see the value he places on you.
Then you know you are worthwhile: it is not selfish to take good care of
yourself. The word of God is as true for each of us today as it was when
first written.*

A reading from the prophet Isaiah.

You will be called by a new name,
one which the mouth of the Lord will confer.
You are to be a crown of splendour in the hand of God,
a princely diadem in the hand of your God;
no longer are you to be named 'Forsaken,'
nor your land 'Abandoned,'
but you shall be called 'My delight'
and your land 'The Wedded';
for the Lord takes delight in you,
and your land will have its wedding.
Like a young man marrying a girl,
will the one who built you wed you,
and as the bridegroom rejoices in his bride,
so will your God rejoice in you.

This is the word of the Lord.

Responsorial Psalm   Psalm 131
A poem of trust in God
RESPONSE: In you, O Lord, I put my trust.

1. Lord, my heart has no lofty ambitions,
   my eyes do not look too high.
   I am not conerned with great business
   or marvels beyond my scope. R.

2. Enough for me to keep my soul quiet and tranquil,

like a child in its mother's arms,
as content as a new born child. R.

Gospel   Luke 22: 24-27
Jesus values you for who and what you are, not for what you do or what you have achieved. He calls himself the servant; he identifies with the weakest of us. His view of us leads us to care for ourselves.

A reading from the holy Gospel according to Luke.

An argument also began between them about who should be reckoned the greatest; but he said to them, 'Among the Gentiles it is the kings who lord it over them and those who have authority over them are given the title "Benefactor." With you this must not happen. No; the greatest among you must behave as if he were the youngest, the leader as if he were the one who serves. For who is greater: the one at table or the one who serves? The one at table, surely? Yet here am I among you as one who serves.'

This is the Gospel of the Lord.

Prayer of the Faithful
Let us make our prayers to God as we offer this Mass:
1. Lord, help us to see ourselves as you see us: you love us and have given yourself to death for us;
R. Lord, hear us.
2. Lord, help people who have very little confidence in themselves, especially people who turn to drugs, to find some self worth;
R. Lord, hear us.
3. Help us, Lord, to value people in our society for what they are, not just for what they do;
R. Lord, hear us.
4. Lord, help us to see the full dignity of everyone, old and young, for we are all children of God;
R. Lord, hear us.

Let us pray:
Lord God, you have made each person in your own likeness
and as they mature and develop,
you continue to create them all their lives.
Give us confidence always in your love for us.
We make this prayer through Christ our Lord.

Presentation of the Gifts
People might bring to the altar 'images of care': a book on care of the mind; health food, care of the body; a friendship card, care of the heart; something to symbolise silence and solitude, care of the self.

Prayer over the Gifts
We bring to this table, Lord God,
the fruits of the earth which you have given us.
You love all you have created.
As we receive the body and blood of Jesus at this table,
help us to know that you love and care for each person.
We ask this through Christ our Lord.

Communion Reflection
Lord God, writes a poet, 'send my roots rain.'

Take time off each day to think and pray,
to care how your life is going.
Give your roots rain.

Take time with a friend to do nothing too important,
but just to be together, to enjoy another person.
Give your roots rain.

Take time to write a poem or grow a flower,
to create something that is something of you.
Give your roots rain.

Take time to play some sport, to read a poem, to pray for a while,
to grow in the different aspects of your life.
Give your roots rain.

For in your roots you find who you are,
and there too you find who God is,
for he has not forced you into his home,
rather he has made his home in you.

Concluding Prayer
We thank you, Lord our God,
for your care for all you have made.
Let us look on everyone through your eyes,
and see each man, woman, and child,
as one you care for and love.
We ask this through Christ our Lord.

20. CARE FOR SOCIETY

Introduction

The theme of our readings at Mass today is our care for society.

We're thinking of the ways in which we live with other people in our cities, parishes, schools, workplaces. The question is, 'Can I make some contribution to making our society a better place, a society of more equality, less poverty, more tolerance, less discrimination, more peace, less violence?'

It's a tall order, but each person can make a difference. None of us, or indeed no group, has the full solution to the problems of society: the problems of loneliness, poverty, lack of faith, homelessness, unequal educational opportunity and many others; but all of us can be part of the solution.

No one person is an island: this is as true today as when it was first written by the poet. Jesus himself made a difference to society by always working for a change of heart in individuals, and in calling for a place of greater justice and equality.

We pray in this Mass that we may become more aware of the needs in our society, more ready to play some part in meeting them, and try to see them with the eyes of Jesus Christ.

Penitential Rite

We ask God's forgiveness for sin in our society, of which we are all a part:

Lord Jesus, you prayed for your enemies; forgive our sins of violence;
Lord, have mercy.

Lord Jesus, you showed compassion and love to everyone; forgive our sins of intolerance;
Christ, have mercy.

Lord Jesus, you plead for all your people at God's right hand; forgive our sins of coldness;
Lord, have mercy.

May almighty God have mercy on us,
forgive us our sins,
and bring us to life everlasting.

Opening Prayer

Lord God, you are present to your people always,
in all places, at every time.

Help us see our people with the eyes of Jesus.
Where there is injustice and inequality,
let us try to spread justice and equality;
help us to build a society
where each person is valued in their dignity as a child of God
in Jesus Christ our Lord.

First Reading   James 2:14-17

*Faith is sincere when it is seen in action. If faith is strong, there will be
activities going with it that make our society more Christian.*

A reading from the letter of St James.

How does it help, when someone who has never done a single good act
claims to have faith? Will that faith bring salvation? If one of the brothers
or one of the sisters is in need of clothes and has not enough food to live on,
and one of you says to them, 'I wish you well; keep yourself warm and eat
plenty,' without giving them these bare necessities of life, then what good
is that? In the same way faith: if good deeds do not go with it, it is quite
dead.

This is the word of the Lord.

Responsorial Psalm   Psalm 103

*A poem about the compassion of God: Real change in society comes from
compassion for people.*

RESPONSE: The Lord has compassion for his people.

1. The Lord is tenderness and pity,
   slow to anger and rich in faithful love;
   his indignation does not last forever,
   nor his resentment remain for all time;
   he does not treat us as our sins deserve,
   nor repay us as befits our offences. R.

2. The Lord's faithful love is from eternity and for ever;
   and his saving justice to their children's children;
   as long as they keep his covenant,
   and carefully obey his commands. R.

87

Gospel
Matthew 9: 35-37

Jesus' care for society is seen in his compassion for the suffering people of society. The Christian follower of Jesus sees society through the eyes of Jesus: people needing care, food, shelter, hope, faith, and love.

A reading from the holy Gospel according to Matthew.

Jesus made a tour through all the towns and villages, teaching in their synagogues, proclaiming the good news of the kingdom and curing all kinds of disease and all kinds of illness. And when he saw the crowds he felt sorry for them because they were harrassed and dejected, like sheep without a shepherd. The he said to his disciples, 'The harvest is rich but the labourers are few, so ask the Lord of the harvest to send out labourers to his harvest.'

This is the Gospel of the Lord.

Prayer of the Faithful
We pray for the needs of the world we live in: for people in need, for a more loving and caring society, and for a continuation of the work of Jesus in caring for society:

1. Make us aware, Lord Jesus, of the need of many people our society for food and shelter, for compassion and for hope;
R. Lord, hear us.
2. Make us aware, Lord Jesus, of your call to each of us to continue, in our own way, your care for society;
R. Lord, hear us.
3. We pray for people who spend their time in caring for the less fortunate of our society, particularly whatever work we do in our own school and class for society;
R. Lord, hear us.
4. Help us, Lord, to be generous in choosing to care for people when we make choices about what we will do after school; give courage to anyone who wants to follow you in priesthood or religious life;
R. Lord, hear us.

Let us pray:
Lord God, creator of our world,
help us, in all our activities and plans,
to care for our society
in the Spirit of Jesus, your Son,
who is Lord forever and ever.

Prayer over the Gifts
Lord God, use our hearts in your work of love
and our hands in your service of your people.
Make of us people who care for the society in which we live.
Grant this through Christ our Lord.

Communion Reflection
People wonder if their efforts to care for society are worth it. Sheila Cassidy gave some years as a doctor in Chile. Tortured, imprisoned, expelled, she wondered was her time wasted. From that question, she wrote her Credo:

I believe
no pain is lost,
no tear unmarked,
no cry of anguish
dies unheard,
lost in the hail of gunfire
or blanked out by the padded cell.
I believe that pain
and prayer
are somehow saved,
processed,
stored,
used in the Divine Economy.
The blood
shed in Salvador
will irrigate the heart
of some financier a million miles away.
The terror, pain, despair,
swamped by lava, flood or earthquake
will be caught up
like mist and fall again,
a gentle rain on arid hearts
or souls despairing in the back streets of Brooklyn.
(*Sheila Cassidy, Sharing the Darkness*)

Concluding Prayer
Lord God, be with us as we leave this place of prayer
to spread your gospel in our society.
May we always cooperate with your care and interest in our world.
We ask this through Christ our Lord forever.

A RECORD OF CELEBRATIONS

The following table might be used to record useful information. By keeping a record of the celebrations you have used, the date, who it was celebrated with, and the time it was held, suggestions for improvement, the names of the celebrant(s) and other personnel, the songs used—you have taken a concrete step toward more effective celebrations.

Date/Time	Title of Celebration	Audience

Names of Personnel	Songs Used	Suggestions/Comments

Date/Time	Title of Celebration	Audience

Names of Personnel	Songs Used	Suggestions/Comments

Date/Time	Title of Celebration	Audience

Names of Personnel	Songs Used	Suggestions/Comments